Calvin Fowler
March 8, 1999

THE INTERNATIONAL MARINE SAILBOAT LIBRARY

100 FAST & EASY BOAT IMPROVEMENTS

DON CASEY

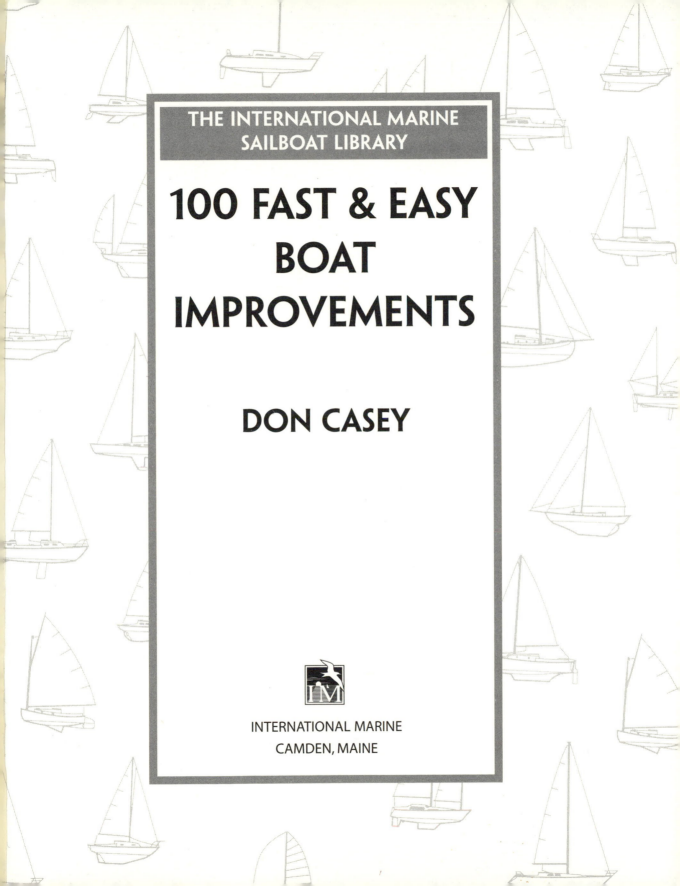

INTERNATIONAL MARINE

CAMDEN, MAINE

CONTENTS

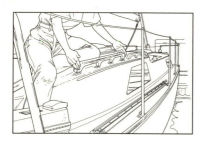

INTRODUCTION

Here was the idea. Gather into a single volume the 50 best boat improvements of all time. Not design innovations or advances in boat construction, but changes an owner can make. And not common enhancements like roller furling and GPS, but ideas mostly new to the reader. The objective would be revelation, not accolade. These would be boat improvements you do at the dock, in your garage, or on your living-room floor, and I would ferret out for you the best of the best.

At first the research seemed easy enough. I took a pad and a cooler and settled myself in the familiar salon of my own boat. All I needed to do was look around to see the improvements that had already made my "great ideas" list. Let's see, there was the compass I had mounted above my bunk that put an end to middle-of-the-night anchor checks. I could include the rack for the pump thermos that provided on-demand hot water in the galley. The little solar panel that had silenced the engine and seemed to make the batteries immortal surely qualified. Seat backs that slide over kidney-high coaming boards made the list. And, what else?—oh, the binocular box at the helm, and.... And...?

It was going to be a short book.

Back at home I dug out a thick file of ripped-out articles and Xeroxed pages. There was some good stuff there—clever chart racks and durable shroud rollers and protective caprail mats made of recycled fire hose—but a lot of what that file contained struck me as uninspired. That seemed curious at first, since I had once been impressed enough to save them, but after a quarter of a century of dedicated messing about in sailboats, I suppose you can't help but become more discerning.

I pruned the file, saving only those ideas that still qualified as genuine improvements. But even as I admired the ingenuity of some of them, I kept going back to a paper-clipped stack of three solutions to the same problem. I had saved them all, but one was clearly superior to the other two. It made me wonder if the other ideas in my file were really the best?

Maybe you can see where this is leading. I was approaching 50 from the wrong side. I couldn't gather project ideas one at a time until they totaled 50 and legitimately call them the 50 best. I needed to start with 150, or 250, or even 500 ideas.

Oh my.

So here is what happened. I went on a mental tour of every boat I had been aboard over the last 25 years—a formidable journey—and I made a list of every notable improvement I could recall. Then I sat down with a stack of more than 100 selected boating books and went through them page by page, searching both text and photographs for good solutions and interesting features. Finally, I did the same with the last 20 years of several boating magazines. When I was done, I had an impressive list of potential improvements. Now all I had to do was pick the best 50.

I couldn't do it. It wasn't just that I couldn't stop at 50. But by what criteria was I going to judge the quality of the ideas, some from sailors with infinitely more experience? Claiming the ones I selected were the best suddenly seemed pretentious. So best was out. Instead, here are *100 Darn Good Improvements*—a suggested title that got darn poor reception from the marketing people.

The title marketing did like—*Fast and Easy*— came from the other two requirements every project had to meet to make the cut. For most sailors there is an inverse relationship between how enjoyable a boat project is and how much time it requires. These qualify as fun projects. Some require only a few minutes to complete and none should take more than a few hours. You need few special skills and only common tools and readily available materials.

I have tried mightily to provide clear and complete instructions for implementing every idea, but be careful not to limit this book's usefulness by interpreting details too strictly. If a particular idea or dimension doesn't quite work for your boat, alter it to make it work.

This eventually turned out to be a fun book to write, but as I whittled away on it I began to feel like the woodcarver Gepetto. Some of the ideas my search uncovered were so irresistible that I found myself doing them rather than writing them. In a way, they came to life. I hope some of them also dance for you.

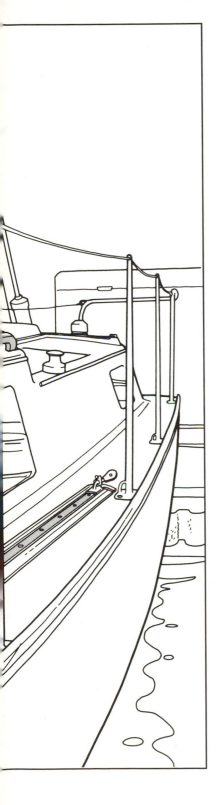

ENHANCING SAFETY

Making a boat safe—and keeping it safe—should be every skipper's first priority. It is of little consolation how exquisite your brightwork is when you're treading water a half-mile above it.

The problem with safety enhancements is that they typically cost a lot of money and provide relatively little pleasure. In fact, despite substantial tariffs many enhancements have no value at all except *in extremis*. The installation of a liferaft comes to mind.

Boat safety needs better PR—Arnold Schwarzenegger mocking wimpy 10-gallon-a-minute bilge pumps; Bill Buckley employing a manual watermaker to disallow the inconvenience of sinking from interrupting salubrious afternoon cocktails. Still, most safety enhancements offer about as much pizzazz as buying life insurance, an apt comparison. As with insurance, you must decide how many of your limited boating dollars to bet on misfortune. The easy answer is "enough."

In this chapter you will find a selection of safety enhancements that, thankfully, avoid this perplexing issue because they don't require many dollars. Several should cost no more than a sawbuck and take less than an afternoon to complete. Yet despite their ease and low cost, these simple projects could very well save your life, your boat, or at the very least the pain of a broken toe.

HANDRAILS

As demonstrated by the old adage "one hand for yourself," sailors have long recognized that moving about a boat is much safer when you hold on. On many modern boats, however, there are far too few substantial handholds. If you can't move from stern to bow and from companionway to forepeak without giving up your grip, you need additional handrails.

SELECTING A PLANK

Although ready-made handrails are available, making your own lets you create the exact configuration you need. Start with a clear plank about 1¼ inches thick—called ⁵⁄₄ lumber. Handrails are almost always installed in pairs, and you are going to make two at once, so your board should be the length of one handrail and twice as wide, not less than 5½ inches. The nearly rot-proof nature of teak makes it the traditional wood for handrails, but you can use other strong woods as long as you keep the handrail well sealed with varnish.

1 Draw a line down the center of your plank. End standoffs should be at least 3 inches wide, so mark their inside edges on the centerline. Divide the space between these two marks into equal segments of about 1 foot and mark the divisions on the centerline.

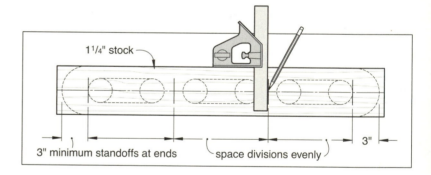

1¼" stock

3" minimum standoffs at ends   space divisions evenly   3"

2 Put dots on the centerline 1½ inches inside of the end standoff marks and 3 inches either side of the equal divisions (for 3-inch interior standoffs). Bore 3-inch holes at these dots, drilling from one side until the pilot bit of the hole saw penetrates the wood, then finishing the hole from the opposite side.

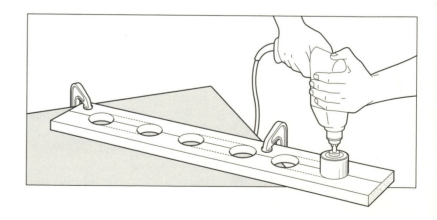

3 Use a sabersaw to make parallel cuts between the holes. Be sure you cut the long distance between holes, not across where holes are close. Also mark and cut the end radius.

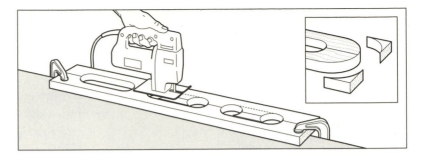

4 Use a ½-inch corner-round bit in your router to round all the edges, including the slots.

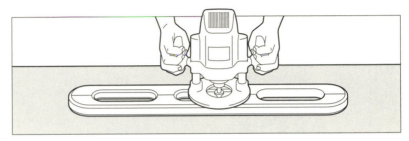

5 Using a table saw or a circular saw with a rip guide, rip the board down the centerline to produce two mirror-image handrails.

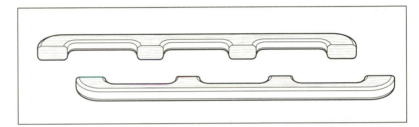

HOLLOW FEET

MOUNTED HANDRAILS will be less prone to rock if the bottoms of the standoffs are slightly hollow. This is easily accomplished with a table saw and can also be done on a circular saw clamped upside down. Set the blade about $\frac{1}{16}$ inch above the table (or base plate) and clamp a fence running in front of the blade at about 30 degrees. The perpendicular distance between the fence and the center of the blade should be half the thickness of the handrail. Run a scrap of material against the fence and diagonally across the blade s-l-o-w-l-y, adjusting the blade height until it leaves about $\frac{1}{8}$ inch on either side of the hollow untouched. When the setting is right, run the bottoms of the handrails over the blade.

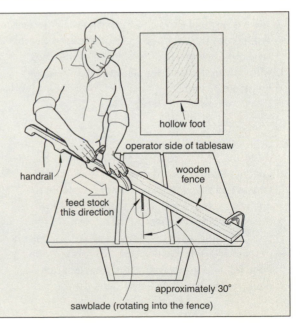

hollow foot

operator side of tablesaw

handrail

wooden fence

feed stock this direction

approximately 30°

sawblade (rotating into the fence)

TRACK PROTECTORS

Actually these should be called toe protectors. Genoa tracks mounted safely out on the rail are generally benign, but jib tracks located in the middle of the side decks are vicious little . . . beasts. If you defang them, there is one less opportunity for snagged lines and injured feet.

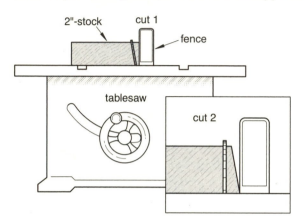

1 Set the angle of your saw blade to rip 2-inch stock to slightly more than the height of your track on one edge and about 1/8 inch on the other edge. Reset the blade angle to 0, turn the board over, and rip out a second strip.

2 Remove existing end caps and cut two strips to the exact length of the track. Sand the top edges flat and round the outside edges. Mount the strips on either side, leaving an ample gap for the car to slide. There is no need to drill additional holes in the deck; simply wipe the deck and the wood strips with acetone or MEK, then coat the bottoms of the strips with polyurethane sealant (3M 5200), and wedge them into position.

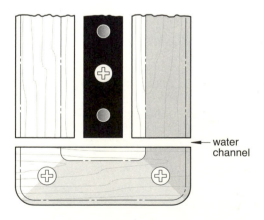

3 Cut short lengths of your wedged strips for end chocks and shape them with a sander. Mount the end caps about 3/8 inch from the strips to allow drainage of the channels the strips create. These must be mounted with screws to allow the addition or removal of cars. Do not bed the end caps with polyurethane; use polysulfide. If you want cars easily removable, caulk only around the screws.

HATCHBOARD LOCK

A hasp and padlock is an inherently weak way to secure hatchboards. A well-placed hammer blow will overpower many padlocks, and bolt cutters make short work of most common hasps. And if the fastener heads are exposed, or if either the hasp or the staple is attached with screws, well . . .

RIM LOCK DEADBOLT

A rim lock is ideal for hatchboard installation because only the cylinder passes through the board; the lock mechanism is external—on the inside of the hatchboard in this case. The deadbolt type is a mainstay of New York apartment dwellers because of its strength; on a boat it not only offers better tamper resistance but also allows you to lock the companionway from inside.

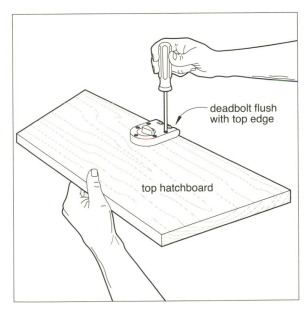

deadbolt flush with top edge

top hatchboard

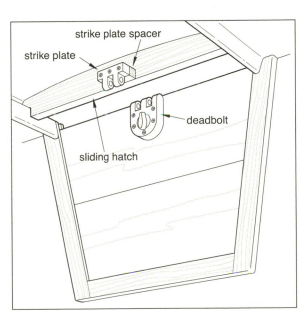

strike plate spacer

strike plate

deadbolt

sliding hatch

1 For the strongest installation, install the lock in the top center of the top hatchboard. Remember that it cannot project above the top edge of the board or it will interfere with the sliding hatch. Follow the manufacturer's instructions for boring the cylinder hole and mounting the lock.

2 The strike plate is mounted on the inside of the sliding hatch. You may have to either mortise or shim the mounting location to get the strike plate to line up with the lock. A through-bolted strike will be stronger than one installed with screws, but to prevent tampering through-bolts must be covered on the outside of the hatch with plugs epoxied in place.

LOW-TECH SENTRY

An alarm system adds a second level of theft protection. Here is one that takes only a few minutes to rig and will at least announce your intruder. Whether it deters the villain is another issue.

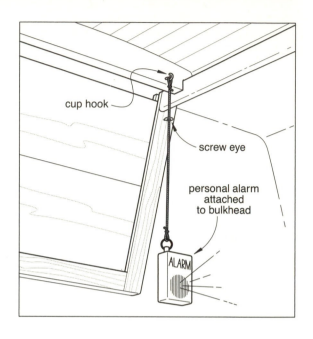

cup hook

screw eye

personal alarm attached to bulkhead

ALARM

For about $10 at Radio Shack you can buy a self-contained "personal alarm" that lets out an ear-splitting 120-decibel shriek when the activating pin is pulled. Mount the alarm next to the companionway and lead a string from the pin up through a screw eye so that when the sliding hatch is nearly closed, a loop in the end of the line will just slip over a hook screwed into the hatch. Install the final dropboard and pull the hatch shut after you arm the alarm.

A string can also be easily rigged to flip a toggle switch. This might turn on the spreader lights at the same time the alarm sounds, or it might activate an alarm horn in place of the personal alarm. Or it can do both. It is a good idea to locate the toggle switch out of an intruder's immediate reach, say inside a locked cockpit locker with the string passing through the bulkhead. If you turn off the main battery switch when the boat is untended—and you should— alarm and light connections should be directly to the battery, with in-line fuses.

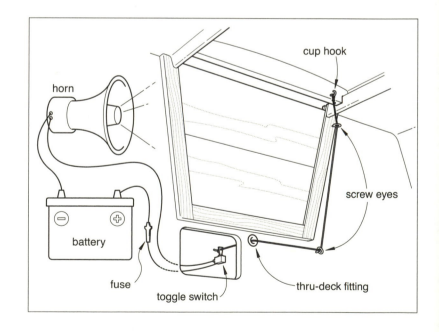

horn

cup hook

screw eyes

battery

fuse

toggle switch

thru-deck fitting

LOCKER LATCHES

Rim locks might also be used on cockpit lockers to eliminate shin-damaging hasps or hold-down clamps, but the cylinders protrude enough to extract their own pound of flesh. A better solution is a jumbo barrel bolt.

WHAT YOU NEED

For this project you need a length of dowel about 1 inch in diameter—an old broomstick is ideal—and two blocks of hardwood about 3 inches square and an inch or more thick.

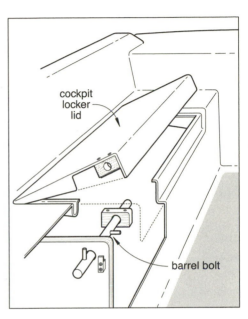

cockpit locker lid

barrel bolt

1 The idea here is to run a barrel bolt along the upper inside corner of the cockpit locker from the hatch opening back through a cabin bulkhead. Latched cockpit lockers cannot be opened without first gaining access to the main cabin, and even then the way to get into them is not likely to be obvious. Exact configuration will depend on the design of your boat, but terminating the cabin end of the bolt inside a cabinet or under a bridge deck is ideal. It could also go the other direction, terminating in the lazarette.

2 After you determine the path of the bolt, install one of the wooden blocks near the forward edge of the locker lid and as near the inboard lip as the lid design and the bolt path will allow. Be sure your through-bolts won't interfere with drilling a 1-inch hole through the block, and use washers and locknuts on the inside to ensure that the exposed (flathead) fasteners cannot be released from outside the locker. A metal backing plate in place of washers provides a stronger installation. Mount a second block to the top or front of the locker parallel to the lid block and as close to it as practical.

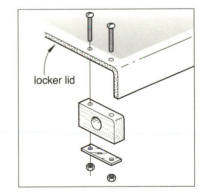

locker lid

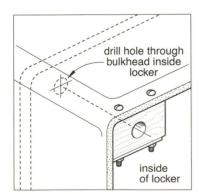

drill hole through bulkhead inside locker

inside of locker

3 Drill a hole through the center of both blocks that will just accommodate your dowel. Get inside the locker, close the lid, feed the dowel through both blocks, and mark where it hits the bulkhead. Drill a pilot hole to check the location in the cabin, then drill the bulkhead for a tight fit around the dowel.

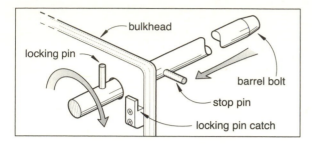

4 Two small dowels glued into the larger one on either side of the bulkhead limit the travel of the bolt and keep it from dropping out of the guide. Friction should be sufficient to keep the bolt in place, but for added security you can install a tab on the bulkhead to capture the cabin-side stopper dowel. Taper the locking end of the bolt to avoid alignment problems.

OFFSHORE LID LATCHES

If you do your sailing on a lake, you can skip this one, but if there is ever any chance that your mast might get below horizontal, expect your lockers to empty themselves—heaviest items first. Many an offshore sailor has been seriously injured by gear flying around inside a tossing cabin. These strong and easy-to-construct latches will keep everything inside their lockers and work on almost any drop-in lid.

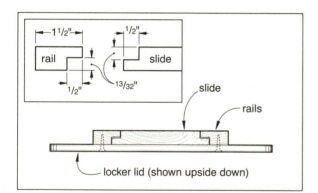

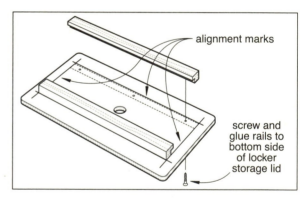

1 Start by making enough rail and slide stock to do all your storage-locker lids. Use white oak or other strong wood. The rail is 1 x 2 (nominal dimensions actually ¾ x 1½) with a ½-inch-wide rabbet along one side just slightly deeper than half the board's thickness—call it ¹³⁄₃₂. The slide is 1 x 4 (really ¾ x 3½) with the same rabbet along both edges. You can do the rabbeting with either a router or a table saw.

2 Lay the one slide and two rails together with ¹⁄₁₆-inch clearance (both sides) and measure the overall width. Half that measurement will give you the distance from a hatch centerline for alignment marks for mounting the slides. Cut a pair of rails ½ inch shorter than the opening—measured between the lid-support cleats—and glue and screw them to the bottom of the lid along your alignment marks.

3 Insert a 5-inch length of slide into the rails, letting it protrude 1 inch beyond the edge of the lid. Glue and screw it in this position. Elongate the finger hole by drilling a second hole on the centerline about 1½ inches from the existing one, then saw away the wood between the two.

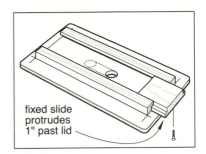

fixed slide protrudes 1" past lid

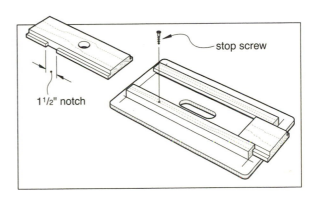

slide

finger hole

4 Slip a length of slide stock into the rails and cut it about ½ inch short of the edge of the lid. With the slide hard against the fixed piece, drill a finger hole through it using the original finger hole as your guide.

5 Remove the slide and cut a 1½-inch notch on one side. Position the slide on top of the rails and mark the location of the notch. Reinsert the slide, then install a small screw through the marked rail to act as a stop and capture the slide.

stop screw

1½" notch

6 You will need to cut and perhaps chisel away a section of the lid support cleat on either side of the opening to accommodate the lock. Install the lid fixed-tab first. Moving the finger hole in the slide from one side of the elongated hole to the other secures the lid.

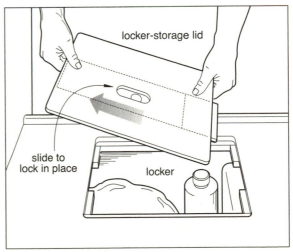

locker-storage lid

slide to lock in place

locker

MAN-OVERBOARD POLE

When someone goes over the side, a man-overboard pole provides an infinitely more visible target than a bobbing head, especially if any sea is running. So why doesn't every boat carry this excellent piece of low-tech safety gear? Because manufactured poles are expensive. Here is how to build one for less than $20.

WHAT YOU NEED

The basis for your pole is two 10-foot lengths of ½-inch (ID) CPVC water pipe. Many plumbing suppliers have it in orange, which is ideal for this use. You also need two ½-inch end caps, a coupling, and a small can of PVC cement. For the float you need 12 inches of 4-inch PVC drain pipe and two end caps. Instead of buying a 10 footer, ask plumbers at the supply counter with you if anyone has a scrap on his truck, or try a construction-site trash pile.

Keeping the pole vertical requires about 3 pounds of lead, which you might also get from a friendly plumber (vent-cap cutoffs) or a neighborhood garage (wheel-balance weights), or you can simply buy economical fishing or net weights. You will need some epoxy to encapsulate the ballast. A 1½-inch coupling makes a good mounting socket.

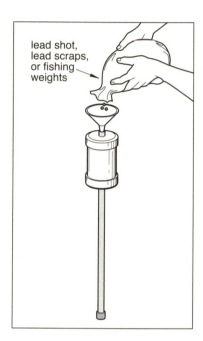

lead shot, lead scraps, or fishing weights

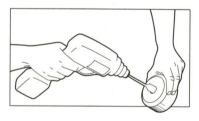

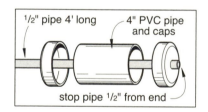

½" pipe 4' long   4" PVC pipe and caps

stop pipe ½" from end

1 Drill a ⅝-inch hole in the center of both 4-inch caps and ream them as necessary with sandpaper to get a snug fit on the ½-inch pipe.

2 Dry-fit the capped 12-inch piece of 4-inch pipe over a 4-foot length of ½-inch pipe about an inch from one end. This is the float. Mark its location, take it apart, then reassemble, carefully gluing all joints with the PVC cement, including where the ½ pipe passes through the drilled holes. To avoid concerns about a leak, fill the float with spray foam or foam peanuts before closing the top.

3 Push an acetone-soaked rag through the short length of pipe to clean it, then cement a cap to the end opposite where the float is located. Pour in 3 pounds of lead scraps or fishing weights, packing them against the bottom cap as tightly as possible. Mix 3 ounces of epoxy and pour it over the lead. If it doesn't cover the lead, let it kick—to avoid excess heat— and then do a second pour.

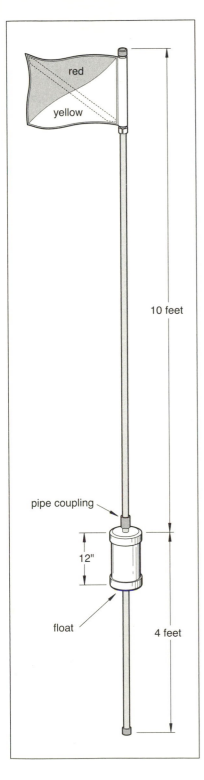

4 To complete the pole, join the 4-foot section to the remaining 10-foot pipe with a coupling. The correct flag is "Oscar," red on the upper outside corner and yellow on the lower inside corner. You can make your own from 4-ounce oxford nylon. About 15 inches square will be a good size, and a sewn-in diagonal batten holds the flag open (see the Sailboat Library book *Canvaswork & Sail Repair*).

5 Double-stitch a canvas sleeve to the hoist of the flag. The sleeve should be a snug fit over the pole. Cut a ½-inch ring from your scrap CPVC and split it on one side. Slide the ring over the pole and cement it 17 inches below the top. Slide the flag over the pole to this stop, then cement the cap to the top to capture it and make the pole watertight.

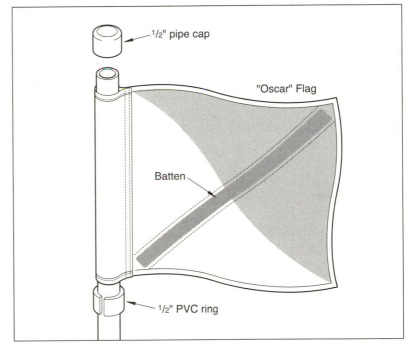

MOUNTING THE POLE

Don't make mounting more difficult than it needs to be. Sew a 22-inch closed sleeve of acrylic canvas (Sunbrella) to capture and shade the flag, leaving enough of the seam open at the corner to allow the sleeve to slip over a terminal fitting. (Put the bottom hem on the outside to eliminate a snag hazard.) Support the mast with a halyard and disconnect the backstay momentarily to install the sleeve. Reconnect the backstay and lash a 1½" PVC coupling to it just above the turnbuckle. Gather the flag against the pole and insert it into the canvas sleeve. Slide the sleeve up the stay and drop the bottom of the pole through the lashed ring. To launch, just lift the pole out of the ring and toss it over the sternrail; the top will pull free of the sleeve.

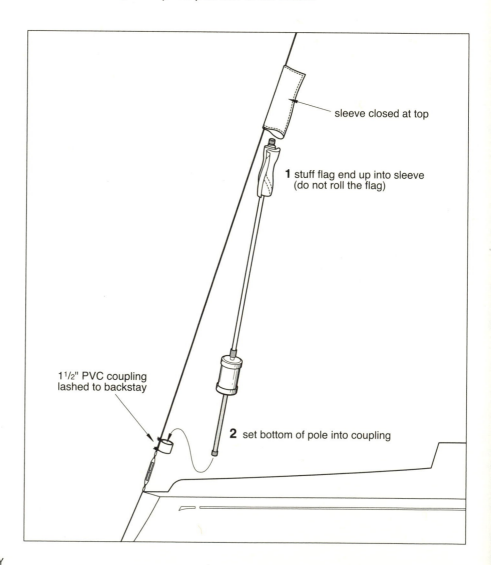

sleeve closed at top

1 stuff flag end up into sleeve (do not roll the flag)

1½" PVC coupling lashed to backstay

2 set bottom of pole into coupling

PROPANE CYLINDER STOWAGE

Propane flows downhill like water. Everyone with propane appliances aboard should already know that propane tanks must be installed on deck or in a vapor-proof locker vented overboard. But regardless of whether you use propane in the galley, what about those disposable cylinders aboard for your torch or barbecue grill? If you have them inside a locker, penetrating corrosion or a faulty valve can silently release up to a pound of explosive gas into your bilge!

MORE PIPE

Since we already have the PVC cement out, this is a good time to create safe propane cylinder storage. A length of PVC drain pipe provides the basis for unobtrusive deck stowage. If you use the long cylinders, you need 3-inch pipe; for the fat ones use 4-inch pipe. Again, scrounging a 2-foot scrap will be more economical than buying a 10-foot length and throwing away 8 feet. In addition to the pipe, you need two end caps, a coupling, and PVC cement.

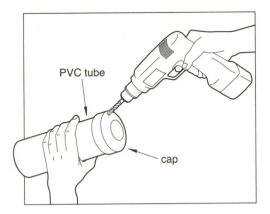

PVC tube

cap

1 Use a hacksaw to cut the pipe to the length you need—about 22 inches for two long cylinders. Glue a cap on one end for the bottom, then drill a ¼-inch drain hole through it—off center so it won't be blocked when the housing rests on the deck.

2 Saw three 1-inch rings from the coupling and sand them inside until they slide over the pipe without binding. Glue one ring to the pipe about ⅝ inch above the installed cap. Glue the other two about ⅝ inch apart and 3 inches below the open end. These act as standoffs and contain the lashings or clamps.

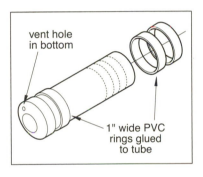

vent hole in bottom

1" wide PVC rings glued to tube

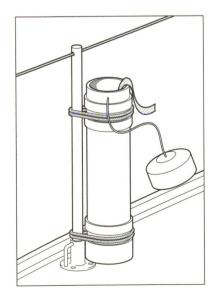

3 Sand the interior of the remaining cap for a slip-fit. Drill a small hole in the center of the cap and one through the pipe just below the cap, and connect the two with a piece of knotted light line. A dab of white caulk reseals the holes. Attach the container to a stanchion or the stern pulpit with lashings or hose clamps, making sure the drain hole sends leakage overboard, not into the cockpit. If your hands are too big to reach into the open pipe, install a loop of nylon ribbon inside the pipe.

LIFE-VEST CUSHIONS

A safe—and legal—boat has a "personal flotation device" for everyone aboard. That generally means cockpit lockers stuffed with a half-dozen extra Type II vests, either on top where they are always in the way, or at the bottom where you would never get to them in a real emergency. Here is a way to unclutter lockers, keep those vests accessible, and improve cockpit comfort in the bargain.

1 Stack two vests and measure their combined length (L), width (W), and thickness (T). The cover is made from a single piece of acrylic canvas cut 1 inch wider than L + T and 2 inches longer than 2W + 2T. Cut strap pieces—two per cushion—3 inches wide and 2 inches longer than L.

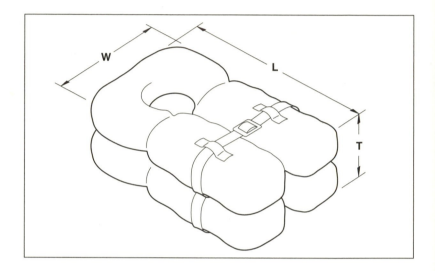

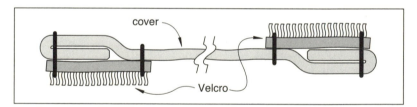

2 Put a ½-inch hem in the ends (the L + T +1 measurement) of the canvas, folding them to opposite sides of the fabric. Sew 1-inch Velcro hook tape to one hem and matching loop tape to the other, hiding the raw edges of the hems in both cases. With the hook tape up, carefully align the loop tape and press the parts together to close the cloth into a loop.

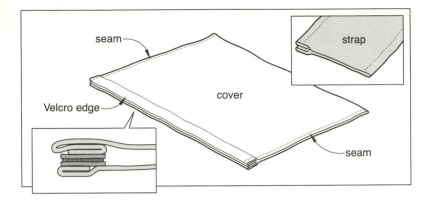

3 Snap the loop flat with the outside edge of the Velcro closure at one crease. Seam both sides of the flat loop $\frac{1}{2}$ inch from the edge. Make straps by folding and stitching as shown.

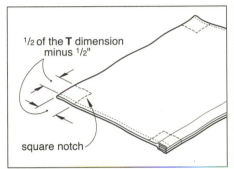

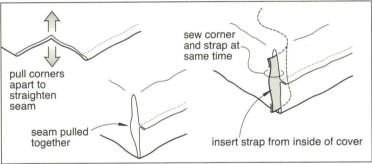

4 The corners are the only tricky part. Cut a square notch in one corner with the equal sides $\frac{1}{2}$ inch less than $\frac{1}{2}$ T, measured from the fold and the side seam stitching. Separate the inside corners of the notch and keep pulling them until the notch becomes a straight slit, then sew the slit closed $\frac{1}{2}$ inch from the edge. But before you sew, open the center of the Velcro closure and position a strap in the center of the slit from inside so your seam will also secure one end of the strap.

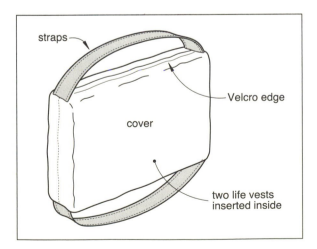

5 Do the remaining three corners the same way, taking care that the straps aren't twisted. Open the Velcro closure fully, turn the cover inside-out, and fit it over the two life vests. They will now serve admirably as a cushion in the cockpit and/or dinghy. The straps make the "cushion" both easier to throw and to hold on to in the water.

BILGE-PUMP LIGHT

The sound of an automatic bilge pump is often drowned out by the other sounds of a boat underway, but knowing when the pump runs can be essential to the safety of the boat. It lets you catch a sudden leak immediately, long before it is under a foot of oily water sloshing across the cabin sole. And the time between cycles is also an effective reminder of needed maintenance, such as tightening a stuffing box.

Any 12-volt panel light will work. Red is preferred, and it should be located where it will get the helmsman's attention when it lights. The face of the bridge deck is an ideal location. Panel lights cost only a couple of bucks, so a second one located in the captain's sleeping cabin can provide welcome reassurance.

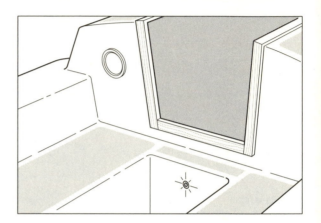

Wiring is simple as long as the pump has a separate float switch. Connect one side of the light into the circuit between the switch and the pump and the other side to ground. When the switch closes it energizes both the pump and the light(s).

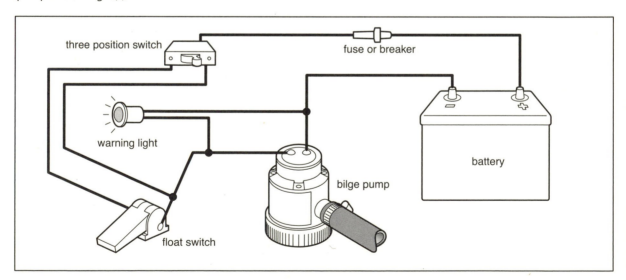

three position switch

fuse or breaker

warning light

battery

bilge pump

float switch

ANCHOR LIGHT/TRICOLOR CIRCUIT

A masthead tricolor running light makes your boat much more visible when under sail at night. And because a kerosene lantern hanging in the rigging can be partially obscured, many enforcement officers find that it doesn't satisfy the 360° visibility requirement for a legal anchor light. Did you know that if you have a masthead anchor light and want to add a tricolor running light, or vice versa, you won't need to run any additional wires through the mast?

WHY—AND HOW—THIS WORKS

Because there is never a need to operate both the anchor light and the running light at the same time, a little clever circuitry allows the same two wires to supply power to both fixtures. The trick is a pair of diodes that exclude one or the other of the lights from the circuit, depending on which direction the current is flowing through the single pair of wires. The diodes you need—capable of passing the requisite 2 amps to the 25-watt bulbs and blocking up to 16 volts—are readily and inexpensively available. You also need a three position (center off) double-pole, double-throw (DPDT) switch.

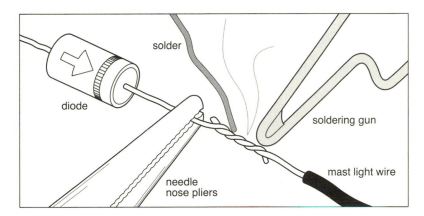

solder

diode

soldering gun

mast light wire

needle nose pliers

1 The diodes will be located at the masthead, so it is a good idea to make up this part of the circuit ahead of time and house it inside the base of the light fixture you will be installing. Diodes are very heat sensitive, so when you make solder connections, be sure you clamp the lead between the joint and the diode with needle-nose pliers to act as a heat sink. Seal the diodes and connections inside heat-shrink tubing, again taking care not to heat the diode. At the masthead you will have to break one of the existing connections and make three new ones.

2 Replace the existing on-off switch with the DPDT switch wired as shown. Flipping the switch one way turns on the running lights; the other way lights the anchor light. The center position is off.

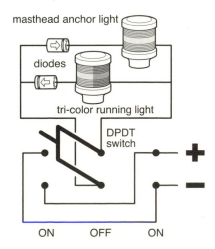

masthead anchor light

diodes

tri-color running light

DPDT switch

+

−

ON   OFF   ON

GROUND-FAULT CIRCUIT INTERRUPTER

Almost everyone knows the likely consequence of standing in the shower and plugging in an electric razor, yet the shore-power circuits on many sailboats are almost as dangerous. Often they don't even include a circuit breaker, depending wishfully on a breaker somewhere in the supply line for circuit protection. But even an onboard breaker, as essential as it is for fire avoidance, offers virtually zero protection from electrical shock. If you are the short circuit, by the time the current reaches the breaker's threshold, it will only matter to your heirs.

WHAT A GFCI DOES AND DOESN'T DO

If you get across the hot and the neutral wires of a circuit, a ground-fault circuit interrupter (GFCI) also will fail to protect you, but most electrical shocks occur when you are unwittingly in contact with only one side of the circuit and touch a ground. In this case, the GFCI senses the flow to ground almost instantly and disconnects the circuit in about $\frac{1}{40}$ of a second—before the current flow through your body becomes dangerous.

Damp surfaces facilitate grounding, which multiplies the shock risk on a boat. Every onboard AC outlet should be ground-fault protected. At less than $10 each, a GFCI installed in every outlet box would still be cheap insurance, but a single GFCI can protect all outlets downstream on the same circuit, so a lot of boats require only one.

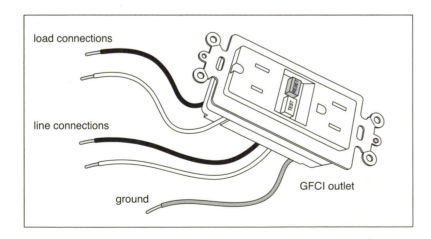

load connections

line connections

ground

GFCI outlet

1 For series protection be sure to get the right type of GFCI outlet—one with both line and load connections.

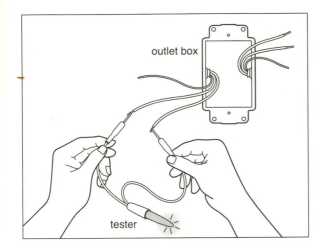

outlet box

tester

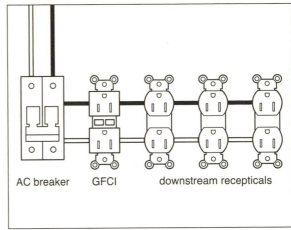

AC breaker GFCI downstream recepticals

2 Unplug the shore-power cord and make sure any other AC sources—an inverter, for example—are disconnected. Identify the first outlet in the circuit and test it to be sure it is dead, then remove the cover plate and disconnect the outlet. With the bare wires protected against shorts, reenergize the circuit and plug a circuit tester into each of the other outlets to confirm positively that this is the first in the circuit. Use the tester to also determine which pair of disconnected wires are hot. Disconnect the power.

3 Connect the LINE side of the GFCI to the "hot" wires—black to black and white to white—and the LOAD side to the other pair of wires that feed the remainder of the circuit. Wire nuts are inappropriate for boat wiring; use crimp splices (or ring terminals if the outlet has screws rather than wires), and for the best installation solder and protect the splices with heat-shrink. Also connect the green ground wire to the corresponding green or bare wire in the box, either with a splice or a ring terminal. Fold the wires into the box and screw the outlet into place. Install the cover plate.

TESTING

Reconnect the power and push the RESET button. It should stay in. Plug in a lamp and turn it on, then press the TEST button. The GFCI should trip and turn out the light. Reset it, move the lamp to the next outlet on the circuit, and test again. Check each outlet to make sure all are protected.

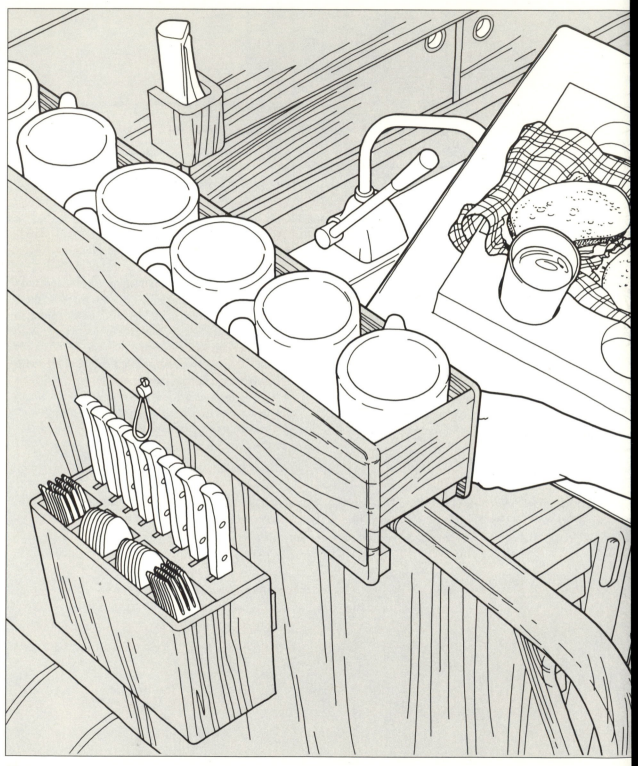

ADDING CONVENIENCE

If you have to climb down the companionway ladder every time you need the binoculars, how long will it be before they are lying loose in the cockpit? But there they are at constant risk of taking a header, so most of us eventually mount a binocular box just inside the companionway. This keeps the glasses handy and out of harm's way, but you still have to leave the helm for them. When you are piloting and reaching for the glasses every couple of minutes, you will appreciate a second box at the helm. Mounting a binocular box in the cockpit is the kind of easy modification that returns dividends every time you sail. Even when it isn't holding binoculars, it becomes a convenient repository for Ray-Bans and BullFrog.

Boats lend themselves to such convenience enhancements. The compact nature of a boat means specific activities nearly always take place at the same location, so it is especially convenient to have all the items you need for an activity right where you need them. Conversely, it can be inconvenient in the extreme to climb around a boat, especially one underway, digging through various lockers in an effort to gather needed utensils, tools, or ingredients.

It is a bad idea to mount a rack where you smash into it every time the boat lurches, but beyond common sense issues, convenience enhancements have few rules. They don't even have to be attractive. Craftsmanship is always desirable, but ham-fisted alterations can be just as convenient. In any case, the projects in this chapter require minimal skills, so you are unlikely to be making apologies. Besides, beauty is as beauty does.

The easiest racks to construct are formed from a single piece of material. For example, a couple of ⅝-inch holes through a strip of teak screwed to a head-compartment bulkhead makes an adequate toothbrush holder (although acrylic is more sanitary). A few holes in a length of angle aluminum create a screwdriver rack. A ring of PVC pipe can be the perfect flashlight holder. Here are three of the more imaginative one-piece racks.

Most sailboats are secured by a padlock, and when the boat is open, the lock is either in the way or, when it comes time to lock up, lost. Even when a handy tray is close at hand, the heavy lock mauls the other contents and invariably leaps out when you pull out your Croakie, denting woodwork and toes with equal enthusiasm. The solution is solitary confinement.

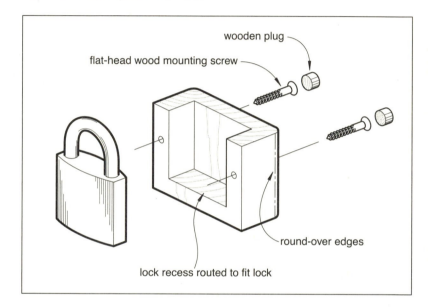

wooden plug

flat-head wood mounting screw

round-over edges

lock recess routed to fit lock

You need a board about an inch wider and a half inch thicker than your lock. Clamping the board on the extra stock, trace the body of the lock onto one end and use a router to remove the wood inside the outline slightly deeper than the lock's thickness. Turn the board over and rout a bullnose on both sides. Flip the board again and cut it ½ inch beyond the routed pocket. Use a finishing sander to round the top and bottom edges, but not the back edges. If you can't mount the holder with screws from behind, center one screw on each side and cover the screw heads with wood plugs. The holder will be most convenient if you can reach it from the cockpit.

ONE-PIECE RACKS: STOVE-LIGHTER RACK

Few items are more essential aboard a boat than a butane match, that long-necked relative to the disposable lighter. They often reside in a galley drawer, where they not only disappear beneath spatulas and spoons, but where there is some risk that the wrong lurch could squeeze the trigger. Lighters are safer and more convenient in an exposed rack.

The construction of this lighter rack is much the same as the lock rack except that it need not be quite as robust. Selecting almost any wood, rout a pocket to accommodate the body of your lighter but leave enough of it above the top for easy removal. Trim the board about ⅜ inch beyond the routed pocket on all three sides. Route a notch in the bottom for the snout of the lighter to pass through. Bullnose all the front edges. With three or four coats of varnish this rack should be an attractive addition to any galley. Just be sure you don't mount it too close to the stove.

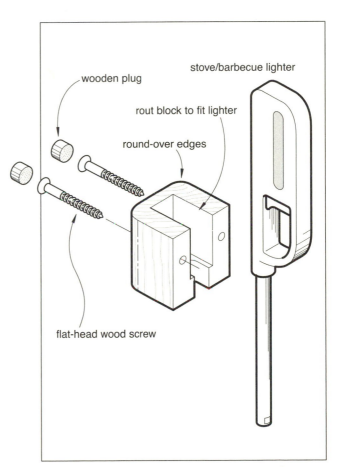

stove/barbecue lighter

wooden plug

rout block to fit lighter

round-over edges

flat-head wood screw

ONE-PIECE RACKS: KNIFE BLOCK

Sharp knives in a drawer can be even more dangerous than a lighter, and banging against other utensils doesn't do their edges any good. A knife block is the solution.

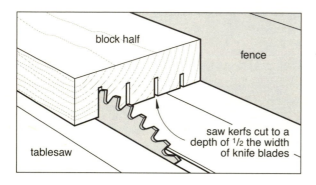

block half

fence

saw kerfs cut to a depth of ½ the width of knife blades

tablesaw

1 Cedar, because of its fungal and decay resistance, is an excellent wood for a knife block. Two-by-four stock will accommodate up to four knives. You need a board an inch longer than twice the length of your longest blade.

Lay the actual knives side by side to determine the most convenient spacing, then cut parallel slits in your board with your thinnest saw blade. For each cut set the blade depth to exactly half the width of the knife blade that slot will hold.

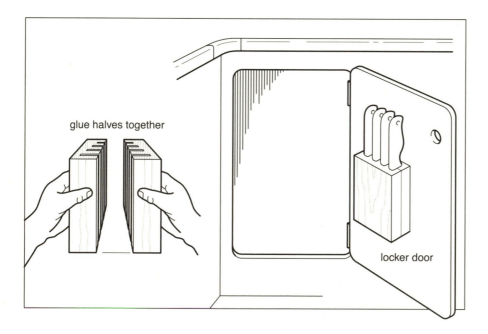

glue halves together

locker door

2 Crosscut the grooved board in half and glue the two halves together, slit-to-slit, to complete the block. The knife block is most convenient mounted in the open, but it is safer to mount it inside a locker—on either the bulkhead or the door.

THE VERSATILE BOX: MUG RACK

The wide array of plastic boxes intended for home use are equally convenient on a boat, and you can also buy wooden boxes intended for specific boat needs. A teak binocular box is the perfect example. However, an ability to construct sturdy, attractive boxes can provide a level of convenience unavailable from commercial products. Here are three box-based projects.

If you've ever tried to serve coffee when the boat was rail down, you will appreciate this clever mug holder. It can either be a permanent feature of the galley or drop in place only when needed—like a carhop tray.

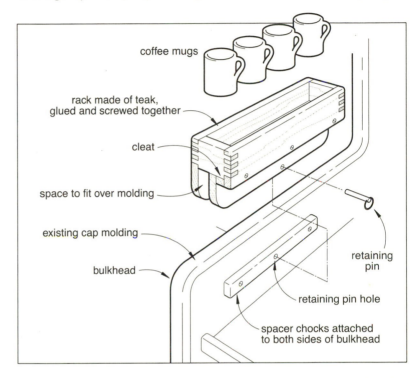

The rack sits atop a partial bulkhead, its exact dimensions determined by the specific design of your boat. If it will be mounted permanently, the existing cap molding should be removed. For a temporary mount, you may have to add chocks below the molding to prevent the rack from tilting. A removable pin through the saddle and bulkhead can secure the rack in all conditions.

Essentially, this rack is a long, narrow box. One side piece has additional depth to form half of the saddle. The other half to the saddle attaches to the bottom at the appropriate width with a piece of cleat stock. How you construct the box depends on your cabinetry skills. This is a wonderful place to show off dovetail joints if you have the tools to do them, but a box built with simple butt joints (glued *and* screwed) does the same job. The drawing shows box joints, strong and easily done with a table saw.

Not only does stowing cutlery in a rack free limited drawer space, it generally allows you to keep the cutlery nearer the dining table—where you use it. Although a cutlery holder can be as simple as sections of PVC pipe fastened to a bulkhead, a wooden rack is more compact and infinitely more attractive.

The best material for this rack is ¼-inch solid stock—teak, mahogany, or whatever wood is appropriate for the mounting location. You could also use ¼-inch plywood, but that will necessitate edge moldings, or at least a rabbet block, to join the front to the sides. Dimensions depend on your flatware, but the maximum width is unlikely to exceed 7 inches.

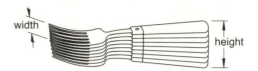

width

height

1 Start by measuring the height and width of the cutlery. A stack of eight forks, for example, is typically about 1½ inches high and 1¼ inches wide, so this should be the inside dimension of the fork compartment. The width of the other compartments can be the same or different as required, but all should have the same front-to-back depth. The height of the rack is about 1½ inches shorter than the longest utensil other than knives; 6 inches is typical. Cut the knife block from 1¼-inch stock. Since it also constitutes the back of the rack, it should be the combined width of all the compartments plus the interior dividers. The depth should be sufficient to fully sheath the blades—typically about 4½ inches. Cut thin, equally spaced blade slots in the block.

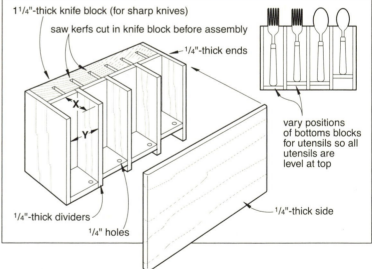

1¼"-thick knife block (for sharp knives)

saw kerfs cut in knife block before assembly

¼"-thick ends

X

Y

vary positions of bottoms blocks for utensils so all utensils are level at top

¼"-thick dividers

¼" holes

¼"-thick side

2 Assembling divider pieces as shown eliminates the need for rabbet joints and encloses the blade slots. First, glue the dividers and the sides to the knife block, then install bottoms in the compartments at varying heights to make all utensils sit an equal height above the top (for access). Bottoms should have a ¼-inch hole to make later cleaning easier. Finally, fit the front piece, giving the joints to the sides an epoxy paste fillet for strength. Sand and oil or varnish the exterior as desired.

THE VERSATILE BOX: SERVING TRAY

The sink cover/cutting board always seemed like a bad idea to me. First, wooden cutting boards have no place on a boat, where sanitation is hard enough without adding porous surfaces into the mix. An acrylic cutting board is safer, lighter, and stows in a $\frac{1}{4}$-inch space. Still, extra counter space is a noble objective. Here is an alternative that truly does have two useful functions.

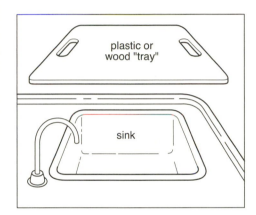

plastic or wood "tray"

sink

1 Start with a serving tray large enough to extend beyond the sink on all sides. This can be a flat tray you buy, a modified cutting board—acrylic or wood—or simply a rectangle of $\frac{1}{4}$-inch plywood with handhold cutouts near the ends.

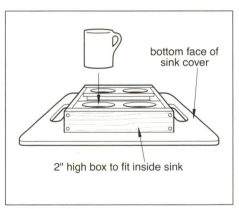

bottom face of sink cover

2" high box to fit inside sink

2 In the center of the "good" side of the tray, construct a box of approximately the same length and width as the sink and a couple of inches deep. For added convenience follow the example of concessionaires and add cup holders at one or both ends of the box.

ACRYLIC BINS

Acrylic racks have the advantage of transparency. If it fits the space you have, an acrylic porthole eyebrow mounted upside down makes an excellent catchall for the detritus of sailing. Otherwise, it isn't that difficult to make bins and racks from ¼-inch acrylic sheet.

STRIP HEATER

Acrylic racks and bins are bent from a single piece of acrylic, and that requires heating the plastic. For accurate bends you need a strip heater, available from your acrylic supplier for about $30. This is nothing more than a heating element that lies in an insulated channel—you build the channel.

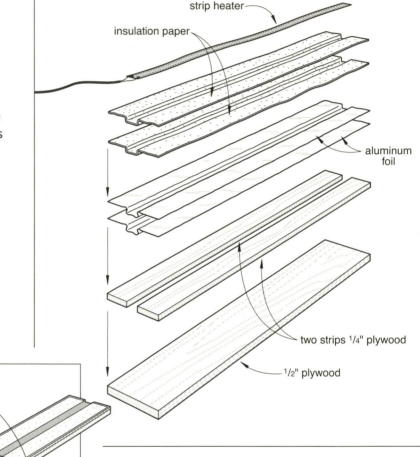

strip heater

insulation paper

aluminum foil

two strips ¼" plywood

½" plywood

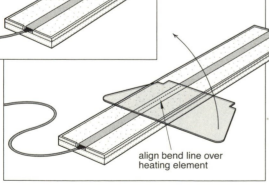

bend acrylic 5 degrees beyond desired bend, then bend to correct angle

align bend line over heating element

To bend the plastic, position the bend line over the heater and leave it undisturbed. It can take the element up to 15 minutes to heat ¼-inch acrylic sufficiently for a strain-free bend. Put a scrap of acrylic over the heater at the same time, and when the scrap is rubbery and soft, your real piece is ready to bend. Holding one side flat, bend the other up about 5 degrees beyond the angle you want, then back it up to the proper angle and hold it steady for about a minute. That's it.

ALL IN THE FAMILY

Whether you need a rack to hold spices or sunblock, charts or cassettes, the basic design is the same. Only the dimensions vary.

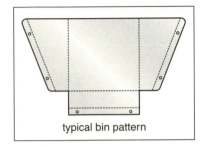

typical bin pattern

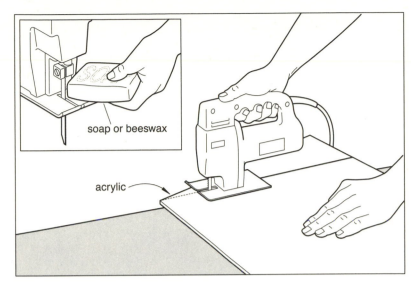

soap or beeswax

acrylic

1 From the illustrated pattern, cut a cardboard mock-up of the bin you have in mind. Fold it and tape it in place to check for size and accessibility. Mark the fastener locations.

2 Flatten the mock-up and trace it onto the protective film covering the acrylic. Cut out the piece with a saber saw and a plastics blade, cutting slowly and preventing the plastic from "chattering." Beeswax on the side of the blade will reduce the tendency of the blade to melt the plastic. Sand the cut edges. Buff them with compound if you want a polished edge.

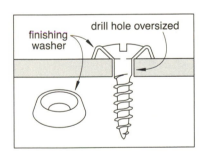

finishing washer

drill hole oversized

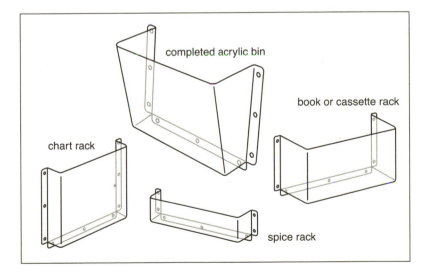

completed acrylic bin

book or cassette rack

chart rack

spice rack

3 Carefully drill mounting holes, using the mock-up as a pattern. Holes should always be a size larger than the fastener to allow the plastic to expand and contract. Feed the drill slowly and never countersink acrylic. Use pan-head fasteners and finishing washers.

4 Remove the protective film and position the plastic over the heating element for the first bend. The sequence of the bends can be important. Bend the bottom first, then the sides, the bottom flange, and finally the side flanges. Get the side flanges right by putting the rack on a flat surface before the bend cools.

COCKPIT GLASS RACK

A solid, secure place to set a can or a glass in an active cockpit is nearly always at a premium. Here is a solution with several options.

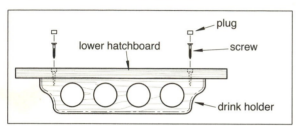

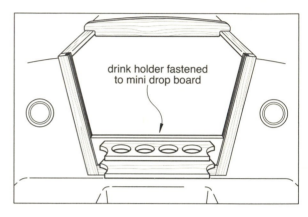

drink holder fastened to mini drop board

1 The easiest approach is to purchase a four-hole teak drink holder from your favorite chandlery and mount it permanently to the bottom companionway dropboard. Aside from the need to step over the board when passing through the companionway, the only real drawback to this arrangement is that it may complicate stowage of the dropboard when not in use.

2 Perhaps a better alternative is to duplicate the bottom 4 or 5 inches of the dropboard and attach the drink holder to this new "mini" dropboard. It will be easier to step over and probably easier to stow.

COCKPIT SNACK TABLE

If you want to build the rack yourself, you need not be limited to a simple glass holder. You can incorporate a snack table or other features particularly convenient for your intended use.

Installing simple brackets at the opposite end of the cockpit will add versatility to your snack table by allowing it to be mounted in two locations. A 3-inch hole saw is all you need to make drink-holder cutouts.

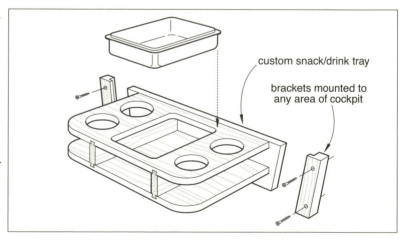

custom snack/drink tray

brackets mounted to any area of cockpit

TELLTALE COMPASS

Absolutely nothing makes sleeping easier than a telltale compass mounted above your bunk. Underway you can get quick assurance that the boat is on course, and at anchor it is a sentinel reassuring you that the wind direction has remained constant.

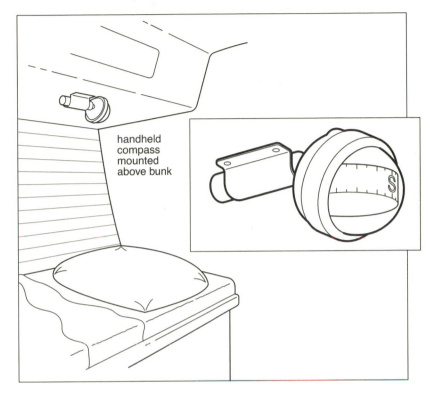

handheld compass mounted above bunk

A compass mounted below has the added advantage of providing a readily available backup in case of damage to the ship's compass. A clip-mount compass like the excellent Silva UN or the Plastimo Iris also doubles as a hand-bearing compass. A "dashboard" compass is less versatile, but also less expensive, and can prove more than adequate for this use. Don't mount the compass near fans, speakers, or other magnetic items.

CHART CHART TABLE

If you aren't away cruising, most of your sailing is likely to be in a limited geographic area. Here is an easy enhancement that makes chart reference instantly available.

WHAT YOU NEED

The idea here is to enhance your nav station by laminating a chart to the chart table surface. For this you need a brand-new uncreased chart. This used to mean a buck fifty out of your pocket, but then Cokes once were a nickel. Chart selection is up to you, but a small-scale "general" chart of your entire sailing area is likely to be the most useful.

You also need a sheet of 100-grit sandpaper, masking tape, a can of spray adhesive (from an art supply store), fresh satin-finish varnish, and a brush.

1 To prepare the table surface, lightly sand it with the 100-grit paper, then wipe it with a solvent-dampened rag. Crop out the most useful section of the new chart, carefully trimming it to the exact size of the table surface. Mask fiddles and/or edge molding and spray the sanded surface evenly with the adhesive. With an assistant holding the rest of the chart clear, position one corner on the table and carefully lay the chart onto the adhesive, rubbing out all bubbles as you go.

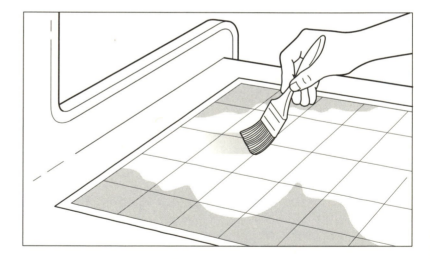

2 Buff the chart with a dry cloth. With the surrounding trim still masked, lay on a coat of satin varnish. Follow with a second and then a third coat as soon as the previous coat is no longer tacky. Remove the masking tape.

CHANGEABLE CHART

If you like the idea of an always-displayed reference chart but you sail beyond the limits of a single chart, here is an alternative that lets you change the surface chart easily.

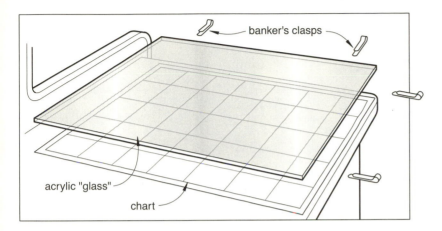

From a picture frame store, purchase a nonglare acrylic "glass" cut to the size of your chart table. From an office supply store, purchase four stainless steel banker's clasps. Crop (preferred) or fold the reference chart to the size of the glass, then clip both to the chart table with the clasps.

HANGING DUFFEL

Duffel bags have amazing capacity relative to their bulk, but being compact doesn't keep them from always being in the way. The solution to getting them off bunks is to hang them. A common location for hanging duffels is against the hull above the bunk, especially above the V-berth where the flare of the hull also carries them outboard.

THE RIGHT MATERIALS

The best material for a duffel bag you carry to and from your boat is acrylic canvas—Sunbrella or similar—because it is strong and water resistant. However, for bags whose primary function is onboard stowage, you can match the upholstery or use any fabric you like, provided it has some mildew resistance. Zippers and slides must be plastic, and twist-lock fasteners and D-rings need to be stainless steel.

You might be tempted to add a mounting flap to a store-bought duffel, but that is generally less satisfactory since it places all the strain on the stitching. If you do take this expedient, be sure to reinforce the bag where the flap is attached.

1 The dimensions provided are for a 2-foot duffel 9 inches in diameter, which can be fabricated from one square yard of fabric. You can, of course, alter the dimensions to suit your specific need. The only "formula" you will need is that the length of the blank for the body of the duffel is 3.14 times the planned duffel diameter plus 8 inches. Give the width and the end-piece diameter a 1-inch seam allowance.

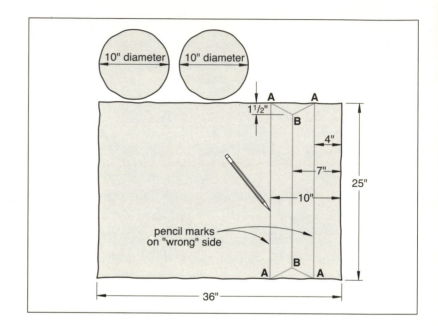

2 Be sure the blank is marked on the "wrong" side as shown in the previous illustration, then fold the fabric along line B-B and stitch from A to B at both sides. Trim the fabric ½ inch beyond the stitching, then turn the flap right side out and topstitch its perimeter from A to B to B to A to A.

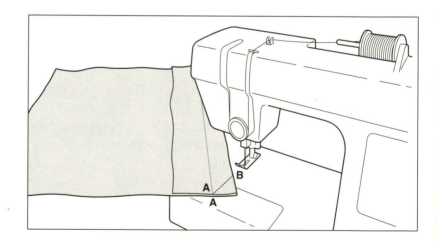

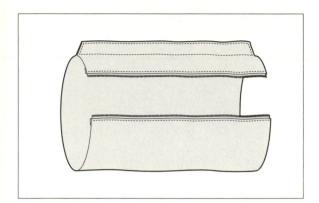

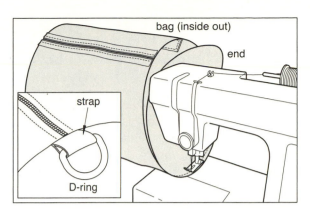

3 With the right side down, fold the 24-inch edge of the fabric back 1 inch. Align the teeth of zipper tape (or one side of a jacket zipper) with the fold and attach the zipper with two parallel rows of stitching. Do the same at the opposite end, taking care to orient the teeth properly so the two halves of the zipper will mesh. Install the zipper slide and zip the ends closed with the wrong side out.

4 Pin or staple an end piece into the tube and stitch around it about ½ inch from the edge. To provide an attachment point for a shoulder strap, fold a 1½-inch length of webbing around a small D-ring and, with the ring inside, capture the webbing in the end seam next to the zipper. Close the other end and attach a second ring the same way. (For instructions on adding handles, see the Sailboat Library book *Canvaswork & Sail Repair*.)

5 Unzip the finished duffel and turn it right side out. Install three or four eyelets in the flap, then mount the corresponding twist-lock fasteners to the ceiling or bulkhead for hanging the bag.

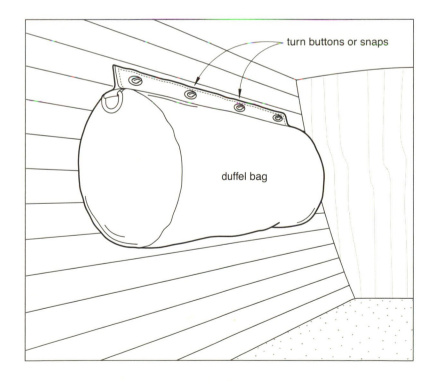

CANVAS BUCKET

It is difficult to find a plastic bucket up to the task of dipping seawater aboard a moving boat. Metal buckets have the strength, but they abhor silence and exhibit a proclivity to do damage. Canvas buckets are strong, gentle, completely silent, and they stow flat to boot, but a traditional canvas bucket requires hours of handwork. Here is a modern version you can whip out in a lot less time.

WHAT YOU NEED

Ten-ounce Dacron sailcloth makes a light, durable canvas bucket. For a bucket 10 inches in diameter and 12 inches deep, you need a rectangle of fabric 34½ x 16 and two 11-inch circles. The top rim is held open with a 10-inch needlepoint hoop, and the bottom gets its shape from a 10-inch disk of polyethylene or other durable plastic ¼ to ½ inch thick. A couple of ½-inch grommets, 15 feet of ½-inch three-strand, some whipping twine, and an office-supply glue stick complete the materials list.

Caution: It is almost impossible to sew slippery Dacron cloth accurately unless you first glue the seams.

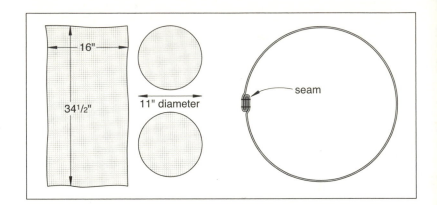

1 Fold the rectangle to place the top edge 1 inch short of the bottom edge and use the glue stick to hold the fabric in this position. Fold the long edge back over the short edge and glue it down. Stitch through all three layers about ¼ inch from the raw edge. Fold the seam back once more and glue it. Open the sleeve you have formed and sew the seam through four thicknesses, placing the stitching about ¼ inch from the edge of the fold. If this seam becomes troublesome as it gets inside the sleeve, sew only halfway from one end, then turn the sleeve around and complete the seam from the other end.

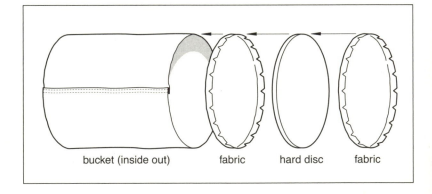

bucket (inside out)   fabric   hard disc   fabric

2 Glue one of the circles inside the sleeve, placing its raw edge ½ inch inside the edge of the sleeve. Sew this piece ½ inch from the edge of the circle. Round the edges of the plastic disk and glue it to the installed bottom, centered. Now sew the second bottom piece into the sleeve to capture the disk.

3 Epoxy the two parts of the needlepoint hoop together, then clip off the metal clamp. With the bucket inside out, slip the hoop inside the open end. Fold the edge over it 3 inches to form a casing. With the first fold glued, turn 1 inch of the raw edge under and stitch the casing down with one row of stitching near the edge and a second forcing the hoop against the top of the fold.

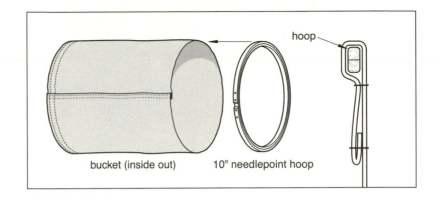

bucket (inside out)   10" needlepoint hoop   hoop

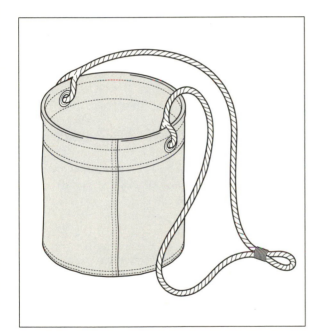

4 Install two grommets opposite each other centered in the triple thickness of the casing. Seize an eye in the center of a 3-foot length of the ½-inch line, then attach the ends to the bucket with eye splices through the grommets. Splice an 8-foot retrieving line through the seized eye in the bail and put a fancy knot at the bitter end as a stop.

ROPING THE BOTTOM

TRADITIONAL CANVAS BUCKETS have a rope grommet all around the bottom edge to protect the boat from the hard bottom. You can accomplish the same thing without the handwork by installing the rope as a welt cord. For a 10-inch bucket, you need 31 inches of rope folded inside a 2½-inch-wide strip of fabric. When you install the first bottom piece, include this oversize piping between the bottom and the sleeve, using a zipper foot to place your stitches tight against the rope. When you turn the bucket inside out, it will sit on the rope ring.

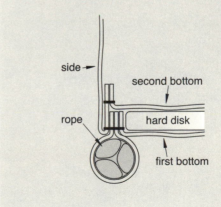

side → second bottom
rope   hard disk
first bottom

DECKWASH/SHOWER

There is a better way than a canvas bucket to get water on the deck. A tap providing pressure seawater is incredibly convenient for hosing off ground tackle, scrubbing the deck, and even for unlimited hot-weather showers.

THE RIGHT PUMP

Centrifugal pumps move a lot of water, but they don't lift it very well. For deckwash use, select either a flexible (or rigid vane) impeller pump or a diaphragm pump. Most marine pump manufacturers offer washdown pump kits that include the appropriate pump, a check valve, a pressure switch, and hose adapters. Such kits start at less than $100.

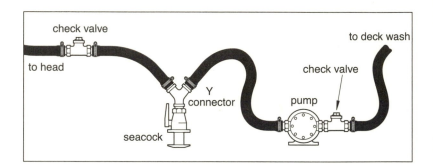

Use a Y connector to tap into either the galley or the head intake line. It is not a good idea to use the engine intake because that puts the engine and the washdown pump in competition for the available flow and because a failure in the washdown pump could cause the engine pump to lose prime. Since pumps push better than pull, you will get the best results from mounting the pump as near the supply line as possible. A check valve on the head or galley side of the Y prevents prime problems and eliminates the need for manual valves.

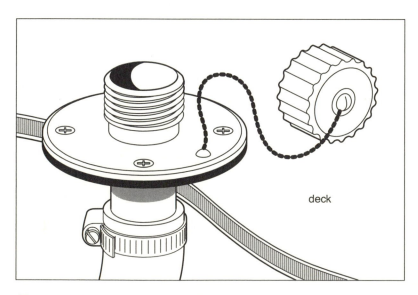

A second check valve is required on the outlet side of the pump to prevent backflow. Connect the pump to the deck outlet with plastic hose. Less obtrusive than a faucet, a male hose connector is normally adequate because flow is controlled with a nozzle on the hose, and the pump is switched off when not in use. One pump can supply multiple outlets, including a recessed shower for cockpit bathing.

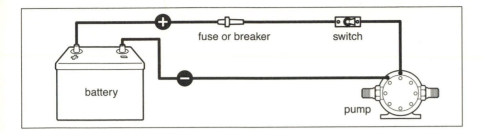

Electrical connections for a deckwash pump are straightforward—positive to positive and negative to negative with a conveniently located switch in the positive side. Because a washdown pump can draw 10 amps or more, you may need a dedicated circuit with a new fuse or breaker in the main panel. If the pump is no more than 10 feet (wire distance) from the panel, 10-gauge wire will suffice; otherwise use 8-gauge, or even 6-gauge if panel-to-pump distance exceeds 20 feet. It is imperative to size the wires properly.

CHAIN SCRUBBER

Some mud resists even the pressure of a washdown hose. Here is a clever chain scrubber that you can put together in an hour. If you don't have a deckwash, you need this even more.

WHAT YOU NEED

This scrubber is built around (literally) three inexpensive stiff-bristle scrub brushes. They are mounted inside a PVC drainpipe coupling (or a scrap of pipe), so the size of the coupling depends upon the size of the brushes you use. The handle connection is a nylon Bimini-top hinge with the matching socket on a broomstick or dowel.

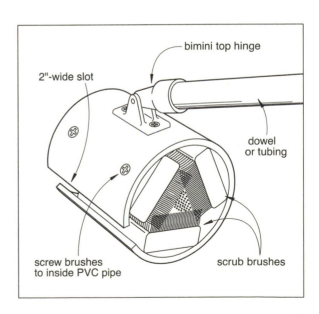

Saw a 2-inch-wide lengthwise section from the coupling. Through-bolt the Bimini-top hinge opposite the cutout. Screw the brushes to the inside wall of the pipe at 120 degree intervals; their bristles should just mesh. Install the socket on a piece of dowel or tubing, then attach it to the hinge. The cutout lets the chain into the brushes, and a little elbow action by the operator strips away even determined mud.

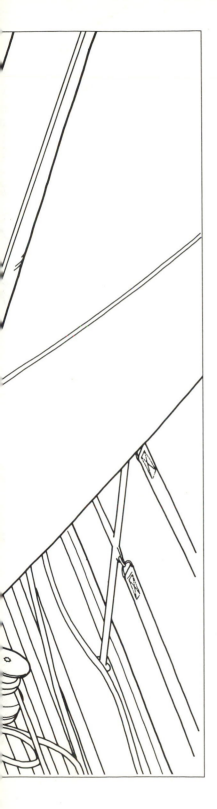

INCREASING COMFORT

I have long thought that any boat with two settees could be improved by replacing one of them with a pair of overstuffed chairs—recliners if the boat is large enough. Add a small side table between them and a good lamp overhead, and it isn't hard to imagine many pleasant hours conversing, reading, or just contemplating the cosmos.

But comfort on a sailboat can be elusive. The best easy chair loses its congeniality when you tilt it forward 30 degrees. And even when the boat lies quietly at anchor, comfort can be easily challenged by the weather, the whine of a mosquito, or a roving shaft of sunlight.

With comfort aboard so fragile, little things take on added importance—a favorite pillow, a reading light mounted in just the right spot, a cabin fan in an otherwise stale corner. Improving padding, light, and air are the primary ways of increasing comfort afloat, and this chapter contains a new twist or two on those essential three, but it also offers a few comfort enhancements that may not be as obvious.

So kick back and consider them all, then implement those you find worthy.

SHIP'S UMBRELLA

I once heard someone describe something worthless as "about as useful as an umbrella on a sailboat." At the time I thought I knew just what he meant. We were both ill informed.

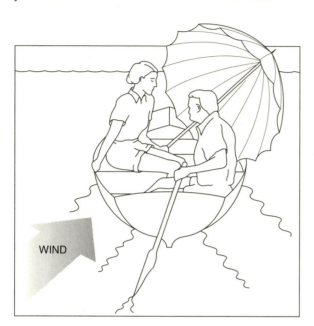

WIND

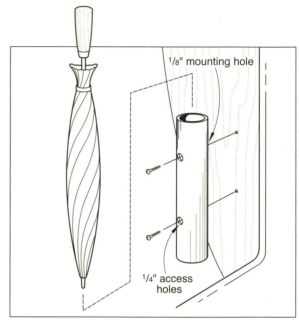

1/8" mounting hole

1/4" access holes

An umbrella makes an excellent spray dodger for those otherwise wet rides in the inflatable. (Forget tradition; you're in a *rubber* boat for God's sake!) It serves the same function in a hard dink if you can get the thing going fast enough to kick up spray, and when you're under oar power, the right umbrella makes an admirable downwind sail. But mostly an umbrella is more comfortable than oilies for going ashore on damp days, and every boat should be equipped with one. The little collapsible kind won't do. You need a big golf or coachman's umbrella, preferably one with 16 ribs so it won't blow out when the wind pipes up.

A ship's umbrella won't fare well in the bottom of a locker and it won't be useful unless you can find it when you want it. A 2-foot length of 2-inch PVC pipe makes the perfect umbrella stand. Drill two 1/8-inch mounting holes about a foot apart. Two 1/4-inch holes drilled in the opposite wall of the pipe give you screwdriver access.

Installing the holder inside the wet locker lets you put the umbrella away wet, but locating it near the companionway may be more convenient. The holder can be mounted at almost any angle short of horizontal.

NONSKID DISHES

A fiddle rail may keep dishes from leaping off counters and tables, but it doesn't keep them from racing around like bumper cars. Here is how to give your tableware a tree-frog grip on tilted surfaces. This works even better than nonskid matting because it is always under the dish.

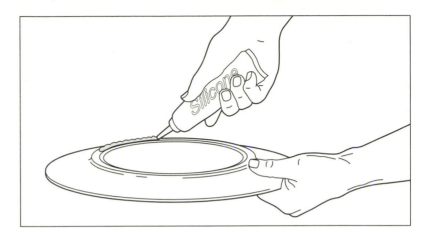

1 Clip the tip of a new tube of clear silicone to allow you to squeeze out the narrowest possible bead. Pushing the bead ahead of the nozzle, apply a thin ring of silicone to the bottom of the dish.

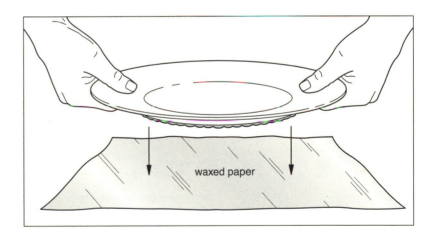

waxed paper

2 Turn the dish right side up and place it gently on a flat surface covered with waxed paper. When the silicone cures—in about 24 hours—it will provide a permanent nonskid "coaster." As a bonus, the silicone ring quiets stacked plates. Dishes can be washed as normal.

SPREADER THUMB CLEATS

Few things are more effective at setting teeth on edge than the clang of a halyard against an aluminum mast. Even the lightest breeze can coax a halyard into a staccato beat, and when the wind really pipes up, most marinas sound like a blacksmith's convention. For the public good, spreader cleats should have been legislated years ago.

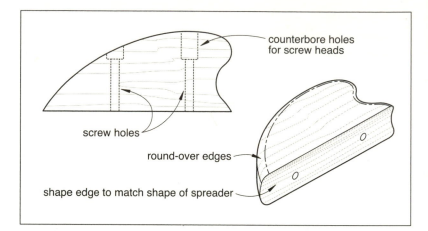

counterbore holes
for screw heads

screw holes

round-over edges

shape edge to match shape of spreader

1 You want this cleat to snag the halyard but nothing else. Cut a scrap of ³/₄-inch teak to the illustrated contour, then heavily round all exposed edges. Hollow the base to match the curvature of the edge of the spreaders. Drill and counterbore two mounting holes.

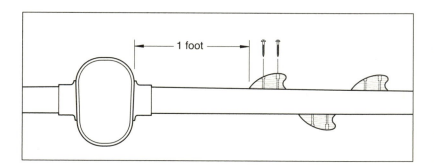

1 foot

2 Screw thumb cleats to both the leading and trailing edges of your spreaders, staggering them to lessen the impact of the fastener holes. You can, of course, install more than one cleat per edge if required. Placing the cleats about a foot from the mast should be sufficient to keep the halyard clear of the spar.

COMPANIONWAY SCREEN DOOR

Everyone seems to have his or her favorite method of attaching hatch screens—Velcro, bungee, chain sewn into a perimeter hem—but none is as convenient as a screen door. Here is a companionway screen you simply push open to go out, it doesn't wake anyone when you open it, and it closes equally easily from either side.

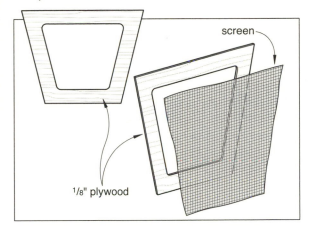

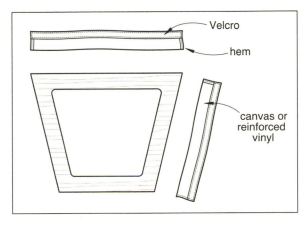

1 Start by cutting two ⅛-inch doorskins to the combined size of your hatchboards, but about an inch narrower. Cut out the centers to form a matching pair of 2-inch-wide frames. Stretch black fiberglass screening (from any home supply store) over one of the frames, holding it with binder clips, and apply a coat of epoxy to glue it to the frame.

2 While the epoxy sets, cut two 2½-inch-wide strips of canvas or reinforced vinyl, one the length of one side of the frame and the other the length of the top (plus a hem allowance if you're using canvas). Hem the canvas on one side and the ends, then sew 1-inch Velcro hook tape to the hemmed edge, covering the hem.

3 Remove the binder clips and trim away excess screening. With the Velcro side down, epoxy one of the strips to one side of the frame with half the width of the strip (about 1¼ inch) beyond the edge. If you glue the canvas to the starboard side (with the screen on the aft side of the frame), the "door" will swing to starboard. If you want maximum durability, now is the time to lay 2-inch fiberglass tape on the screened frame and saturate it with epoxy. When the epoxy kicks, coat the mating surfaces of both frames with slightly thickened epoxy and clamp them together, sandwiching the screening (and the fabric). Binder clips will again serve.

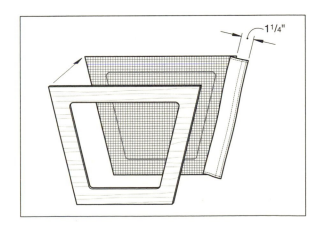

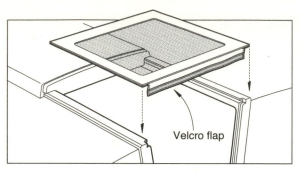

Velcro flap

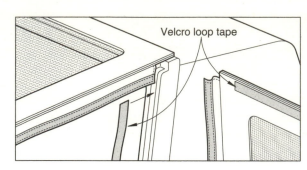

Velcro loop tape

4 Measuring the distance from outside to outside of the hatch slides, and from the open hatch to the top of the dropboards, follow the same procedure to build a second framed screen that size, including the second canvas strip centered at the aft edge.

5 Glue a matching strip of 1-inch Velcro loop tape to the inside top of the dropboard screen. Glue a second strip of Velcro loop tape inside the starboard dropboard channel. The tape goes either in the bottom of the channel or on the part the boards rest against when you push them from outside. Most channels have ample depth or width to accommodate the Velcro without interfering with dropboard installation, but if not you will need to rout or sand.

6 Press the hook tape on the canvas to the loop tape in the channel to provide a canvas hinge on one side of the screen. When you close the screen the first time, if it hangs up on the outside rail of the channel, trim the loose edge to make it clear.

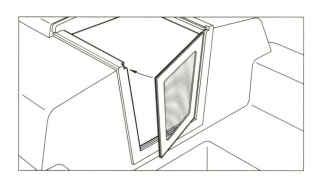

7 From inside the cabin, lay the top screen on the slide rails with the Velcro up and press it to the matching loop tape on the dropboard screen. To leave the cabin simply push up and out and the screens swing open. Swing them back and lower the top to close them behind you. A knob is not a good idea because it will prevent you from storing these screens under a bunk, but a knotted cord through a drilled hole serves well as a pull. If you need to close the sliding hatch, for rain perhaps, simply remove the top screen (which is why it attaches with Velcro) and use the "door" alone. Any gap between the screen and the hatch can be closed with foam weather stripping (on the hatch).

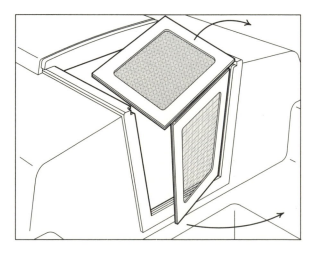

CURTAINS

Cabin curtains aren't just about appearance, or even privacy. They also contribute to comfort. As the boat swings, sun beaming through the portlights, no matter how small they are, sweeps the cabin like prison-yard spotlights until it locates your face. There is no escape.

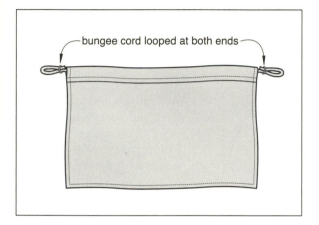

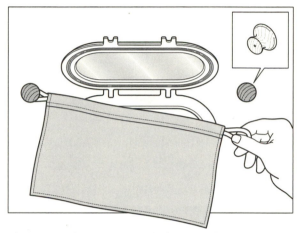

Block-out curtains are easily made from the fabric of your choice by hemming three sides and putting a casing—a hem with both ends open—on the fourth. Thread light bungee through the casing and hog-ring or whip eyes on both ends.

Elegant attachments are made from small drawer knobs epoxied on either side of the portlight at the height of the hinges. Install the curtain by slipping the loops over the knobs. This curtain can be used with the port open or closed.

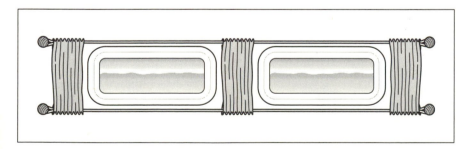

The same "rod" system works equally well for permanently installed curtains over the fixed ports in the main salon. In this case use four knobs, the second set mounted below the deadlights. The knobs should also be far enough beyond the ends of the ports to allow ruffled curtains to gather beyond the glass when they are open.

EYEBROW AWNINGS

The patter of rain on deck, day or night, sends you scrambling to close hatches and portholes. Then, while you wait anxiously for it to stop, temperature and humidity in the cabin soar. Eyebrow awnings have the significant comfort advantage of allowing the portholes to remain open in rain, and they block direct sunlight as well as curtains do.

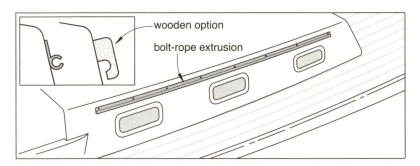

1 Install a bolt-rope extrusion above the portholes you want to cover. If you find an aluminum extrusion objectionable, two passes with a router configures a wooden eyebrow to accept a bolt rope. Such an eyebrow traditionally runs the length of the deckhouse.

2 Make eyebrow awnings from acrylic canvas. A single awning might cover one, two, or all the ports on one side of the boat. It should be as wide as possible without blocking passage on the side deck. Hem three sides and sew a ⅛-inch bolt rope into the fourth. Corner grommets (and intermediate ones if the awning is long) complete the job.

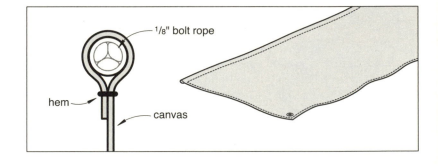

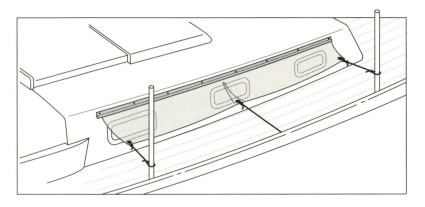

3 Rigged awnings should slant downward as much as possible without interfering with your view through the port. Tie the grommet lines to the lower lifeline, the toe rail, or purpose-installed strap eyes. For easier installation, use bungee rigged with S hooks.

PUSHPIT SEAT

Pushpit seats are all the rage at boat shows these days, and they are great when the boat is going down-wind. Whether you can easily add them to your boat depends on the configuration of the sternrail. Here is a starting point.

1 At the level of the lower lifeline, measure the triangle formed by the three sternrail supports nearest the "corner" of the pulpit. Since many sternrails have only four supports, one may well be across the boat's centerline from the subject corner, but that is usually OK.

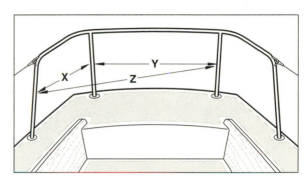

2 Cut a piece of acrylic canvas to the measured dimensions and put a 1½-inch double hem in all three sides. Install grommets in the three corners.

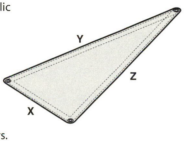

3 Lash the canvas triangle drum-tight with rolling hitches. If the supports tilt apart at the bottom, the lashings will be unlikely to slide. A second seat can be rigged for the opposite corner; the overlap of the two is usually of no consequence.

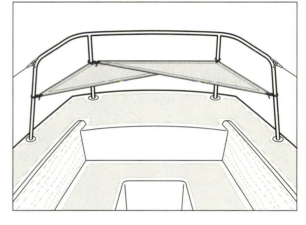

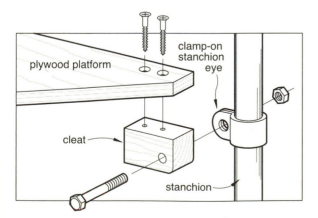

4 If you prefer a solid seat, drill corner holes in a triangular board and lash it the same way. For a rigid mount, use clamp-on stanchion eyes.

Lifelines around the cockpit are sometimes convenient for back support, but they're never comfortable. Fortunately, wire isn't the only choice for lifelines. Two-inch nylon webbing has approximately the same strength as $^3/_{16}$-inch stainless steel wire.

WHAT KIND OF WEBBING?

You want nylon or polyester (Dacron) webbing, not polypropylene. From your nearest wrecking yard you should be able to get all the webbing you need in almost any color for a couple of bucks. I prefer this "factory" seat belt webbing because it has to meet rigorous test standards, but buy new webbing if you feel better about it. Two-inch provides both strength and comfort.

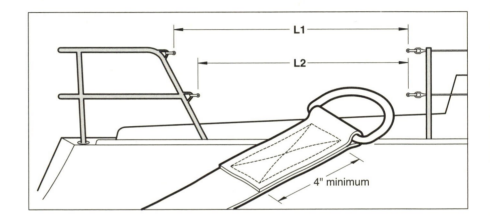

1 Determine the shackle-to-shackle length your finished section of lifeline needs to be, then loop the webbing through welded D-rings or triangles to give you that length. The ends should overlap at least 4 inches. Sew them with an X-box stitch using strong polyester thread.

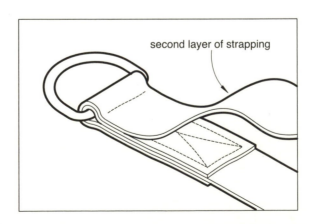

second layer of strapping

2 Thin webbing will be more comfortable and, of course, stronger if you double it. Sew one piece around the D-ring, then pass the end of the other through from the opposite direction and stitch it. Sew the edges of the two pieces together.

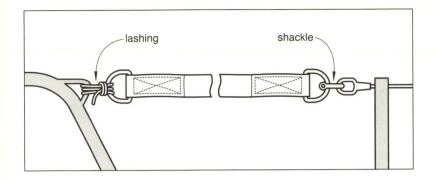

3 If the webbing lifelines attach directly to wire ones, use shackles as strong as the D-rings. Where they fasten to stanchions (or the sternrail) at both ends, a lashing at one end will allow tensioning. Both nylon and polyester deteriorate in the sun, so webbing lifelines should be replaced every two or three years.

COCKPIT SEAT BACKS

While solid wood cockpit coamings help give many older boats their "classic" good looks, they are invariably too short to provide comfortable cockpit seating. But before you start thinking too seriously about trading for something with high, molded coamings, give this solution a try.

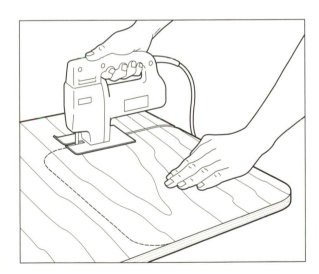

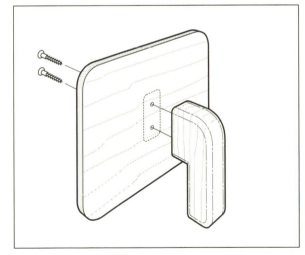

1 For a painted back, start with a foot square of ³⁄₈-inch plywood. If you prefer it finished bright, make your own "mahogany" plywood from squares of doorskin laminated together with epoxy. Round the corners and sand the edges.

2 Cut the illustrated "hook" from stock at least a full inch thick, shape it with a sander, and attach it to the center of one edge with screws through the plywood. The assembly should slip loosely over the coaming. Take it apart and reassemble with epoxy.

3 Paint or varnish the seat back and glue protective leather inside the hook and on the back where it rests against the coaming. Stop here if you just want support for a loose cushion.

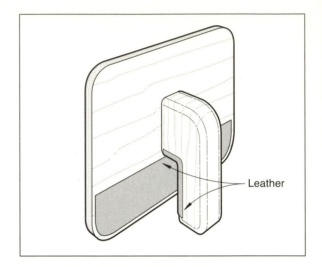

Leather

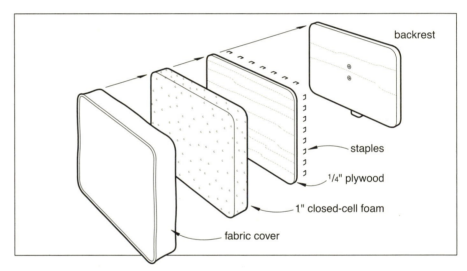

backrest

staples

1/4" plywood

1" closed-cell foam

fabric cover

4 For a padded backrest, cut and round a piece of 1/4-inch plywood to match the seat back. Glue 1-inch closed-cell foam to the plywood and upholster this pad by wrapping acrylic canvas onto the plywood and stapling it with 1/4-inch Monel staples. Or, for a more professional look, use 2-inch foam, and box and pipe the cover. Glue the pad to the back with epoxy.

GRATE BERTH

Traditional cockpit gratings, as lovely as they are to look at, are hard on bare feet. A slat-style grating is both more comfortable and easier to construct, and it has the considerable added advantage that it easily converts your cockpit into a star-canopied king-size bed.

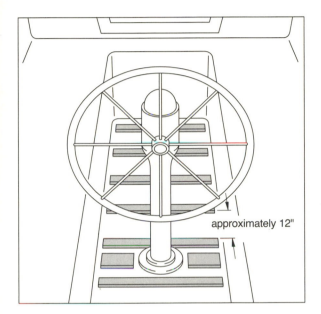

approximately 12"

GOOD WOOD

Two-inch slats are ideal, but plain 1 x 2 ($^3/_4$ inch by 1$^1/_2$ inch actual dimensions) works nearly as well. Use teak, or reduce the cost considerably by using redwood, red cedar, or even yellow pine. Rout (or sand) a $^1/_4$-inch radius on the edges of the slats.

1 Using the slat stock, cut crosspieces to the sole width as close to both ends of the cockpit as possible without interfering with the drains. Cut intermediate crosspieces located about every 12 inches. If the cockpit is interrupted with a steering pedestal or a mizzenmast, place a crosspiece both forward and aft of the base (or step), and short 1 x 4 crosspieces in line with its center.

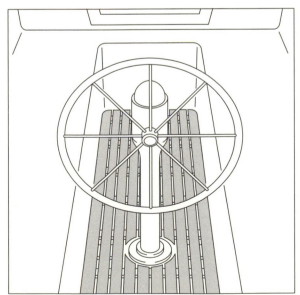

2 Cut slats to the length of the sole and position them $^1/_4$ inch apart on top of the crosspieces. Cut the outside slats to accommodate side taper, but if this requires trimming the slats to less than about $^3/_4$ inch wide, replace the outside two slats (on both sides) with a 1 x 4 trimmed to fit. Center slats may be discontinuous because of the pedestal or mast.

3 Carefully mark the sequence of the slats and the locations of the crosspieces, then remove the wood from the cockpit and assemble it with #8 x 1¼ brass flathead wood screws driven through the crosspieces. Drill pilot holes for the screws to avoid splitting. If you coat mating surfaces with epoxy, one screw at each intersection will be sufficient, except for the crosspieces on either side of the pedestal.

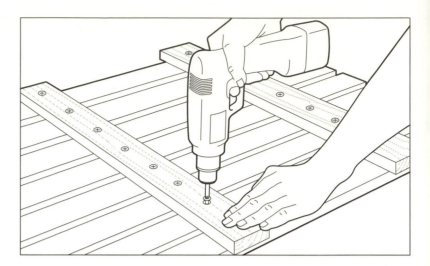

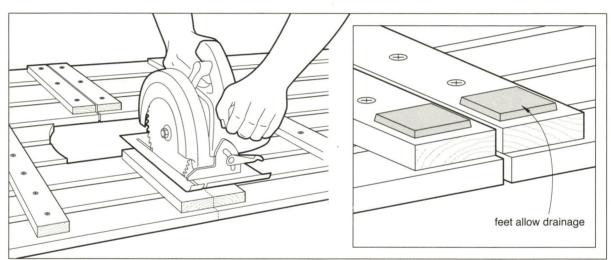

feet allow drainage

4 If the grating fits around a pedestal, cut it into two pieces as shown. Glue ⅛-inch wood, plastic, or rubber "feet" to the bottom of the crosspieces to lift them for drainage.

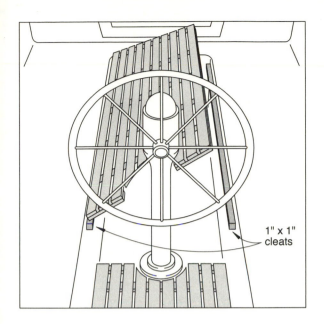

1" x 1"
cleats

5 Install 1 x 1 cleat stock on the sides of the cockpit
1½ inches below the level of the seats. When these
cleats support the grate at seat level, cushions from
below make it into a spacious and cool outdoor
bunk. Otherwise, the grate provides a dry and gentle
cockpit sole.

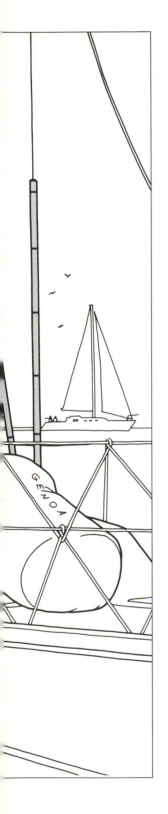

BETTER SAILING

Nothing really makes you a better sailor except going sailing. Practice is what cures oversteering, what makes tacks sharp, what teaches you when you are giving up more in speed than you are gaining in direction.

Better *sailing* is a different thing. It implies only pleasure, not skill. If you want to go faster and you do, that is better sailing, but if you simply avoid some problem that could sully the peacefulness of being windborne, that also is better sailing.

There are few practical reasons to set off across a body of water in a boat powered by the wind. Motivations are internal. It is the artistry of sailing that attracts most, a way for burly men to safely embrace poetry. Others are drawn by its contrast to the high speed of life ashore—escape, for lack of a better term. For some the pleasure is in the challenge; for others it is in the solitude. Sometimes the allure isn't the sailing at all, but simply what is beyond the horizon.

Whatever your reason for sailing, this chapter provides easy-to-implement solutions to a number of common vexations when a sailboat is underway. Some of these will surely make your sailing better.

RIGGING ROLLERS

Letting your headsails drag across shrouds on every tack is hard on the sails. It also results in a sloppy looking tack when the clew hangs up, and can occasionally require someone to go forward to manually release the backwinded sail. Shroud rollers solve these problems, but plastic rollers get brittle in the sun and can eventually represent more risk than relief. Wooden rollers last forever.

WHAT YOU NEED

Make these rollers from half-round molding purchased from your local lumber yard. Both oak and ash are good choices; you need two 6-foot lengths for each roller. Required tools are a router, a core box bit slightly larger than the wire diameter, and a ½-inch straight bit. You will also need epoxy, varnish, a Scotchbrite pad, and waxed twine.

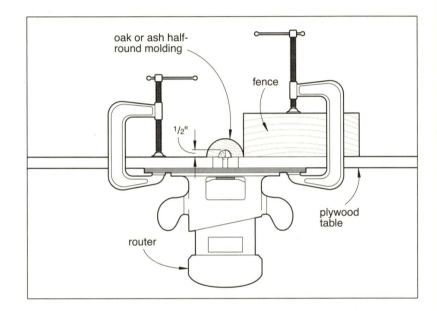

1   Chuck the core box bit into your router. A router table is handy for this project, but if you don't have one, clamp the router to a foot square of scrap plywood and plunge the bit through this "table." Support the plywood with the router underneath and set the bit height to exactly half its diameter. Clamp a fence next to the bit so that the distance from the center of the bit to the fence is exactly half of your molding diameter. Keeping the molding tight against the fence, run every piece over the bit to put a half-round groove in its center.

2 Mate the two halves, reversing one if necessary to match the grooves, then tape them together in several places with a single thickness of tape. Without removing the router or the fence from the table, replace the core box bit with the $\frac{1}{2}$-inch straight bit, plunge it through the table, then set it to a height of $\frac{1}{16}$ inch. By pushing the assembled roller across the cutter and against the fence, then slowly rotating the roller, you can cut perfect $\frac{1}{16}$-inch deep channels right around the rollers. Assuming a 72-inch roller, cut channels $2\frac{1}{4}$ inches (to the center) from each end, then four more equally spaced on $13\frac{1}{2}$-inch centers.

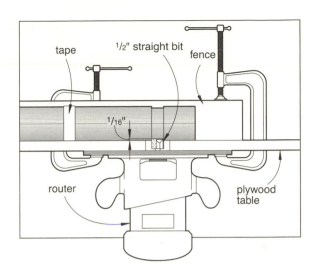

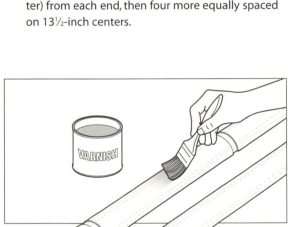

3 Take the halves apart and code them inside so you can quickly tell which two are mates. Lightly sand, then give the halves two or three coats of epoxy to seal them. Let the epoxy cure overnight. Epoxy is not UV resistant, so after you scrub the waxy film off with a Scotchbrite pad and water, lay several coats of varnish (or paint if you prefer) on top of it.

4 Split a stainless steel washer and fit it over the wire, resting it against the top of the terminal fitting to act as a bearing. Assemble the roller on the wire and tape the halves together. Whip them together permanently with the waxed twine in the routed channels—tightly—then remove the tape.

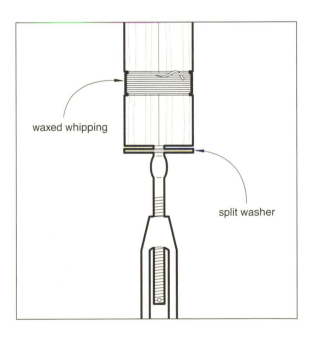

BOW NETTING

Netting laced to the lifelines is usually meant to keep pets or children aboard, but at the bow it does the same for doused sails. Here is an unobtrusive jib net that minimizes windage.

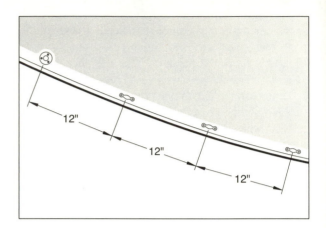

1 Directly below the lifelines attach small eye straps to the deck on 12-inch centers.

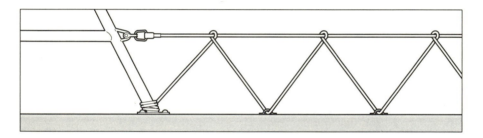

2 Starting at the base of the pulpit, lace $1/8$-inch braided nylon cord over the lower lifeline and through each eye, throwing a half hitch in the cord as it passes over the lifeline.

3 Lace a second cord through the lower lacing and over the upper lifeline, putting in half hitches on the upper lifeline. Tie the end off with a rolling hitch and whip it.

DOWNHAUL

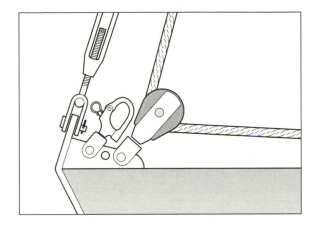

E fficient roller-furling systems have all but re-placed hank-on sails, but if you have resisted this trend, or you hoist a jib on an inner stay, or you fly a hank-on sail for any reason, a downhaul makes dousing the sail as easy as roller furling—with less opportunity for trouble.

1 Shackle or seize a block to the stay fitting at the deck, or attach it to a padeye installed for this purpose.

2 Splice a length of ¼-inch soft-lay three-strand line to the eye in the shackle end of the halyard. Also pass a screw shackle through the eye and around the stay. If you handle the halyard from the mast, lead the downhaul through the block and back along the deck to a cleat near the mast, using fairleads or turning blocks if necessary. If your halyards lead into the cock-pit, take the downhaul there.

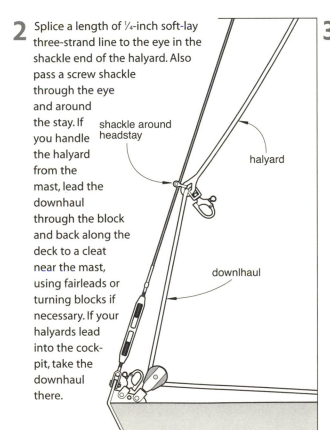

shackle around headstay

halyard

downlhaul

3 The downhaul should be long enough to allow the full hoist of the halyard with the end of the downhaul secured to the cleat. Attaching the hanks on alternating sides of the downhaul "weaves" it against the luff and minimizes chafe. Let the downhaul run and haul on the halyard to hoist the sail. Let the halyard run and haul on the downhaul to douse it.

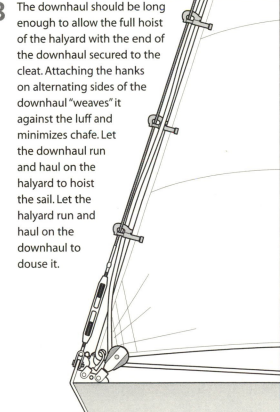

Nothing will improve your docking technique more than a midships cleat. Get a line ashore from that cleat and you can come to the dock parallel and completely under control.

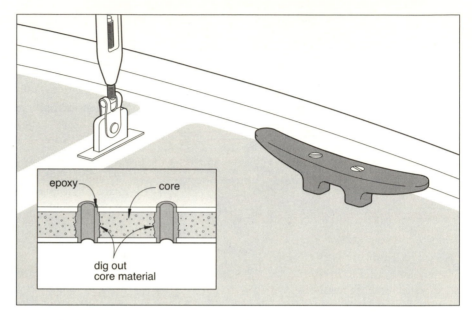

epoxy   core

dig out
core material

A midship cleat is best located on the inside of a bulwark, but if it has to go on the deck, position it as near the rail as possible to minimize stubbed toes and snagged lines. In a cored deck, drill mounting holes oversize, fill them with epoxy to seal the core, then drill through the center of the epoxy plug.

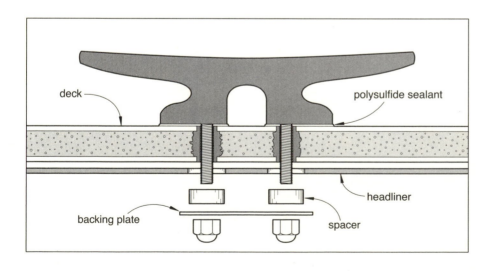

deck

polysulfide sealant

headliner

backing plate

spacer

Bed the cleat and the mounting bolts in poly-sulfide. Through-bolt the cleat and use a backing plate on the underside of the deck.

CLEAT BLOCKS

Good deck cleats are essential for docking and anchoring, but they are nothing but a nuisance under sail. Here is how to make snagged sheets a thing of the past.

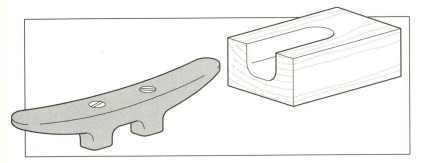

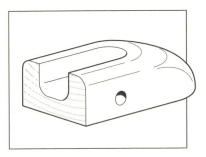

1 Start with two blocks of any durable wood. They must be as tall as the cleat, as wide as its base, and twice the length of a horn. Begin by carving—with chisel, router, or rotary tool (Dremel)—the top of each block to cradle the horn.

2 With a sander, plane, or whittling knife, shape the blocks like the end of a canoe. Drill a 1/4-inch hole through both blocks as shown, then counter-bore one hole about an inch with a 3/8-inch bit.

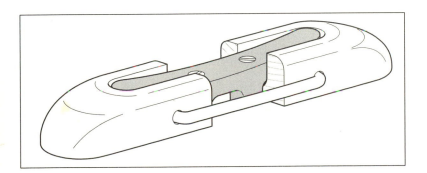

3 Varnish or paint the blocks as you prefer, then connect them with a bungee passed through both drilled holes and knotted into a loop. Pull the knot into the counterbore. The bungee holds the blocks in position but makes them easily removable when you need the cleat.

BLOCK SILENCERS

Banging blocks are hard on the deck and hard on the nerves, and they disturb the off watch. Here are two ways to quiet them.

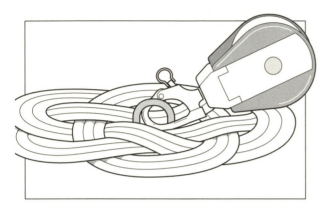

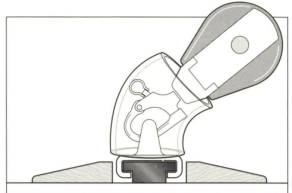

1 For blocks attached to a padeye, put a ropework mat over the eye before attaching the block. It dresses up the eye and cushions the block. The thump mat shown is a flat three-strand Turk's head.

2 Blocks shackled to track cars or padeyes can be kept from banging with a short piece of thick-walled hose. The diameter must be large enough to allow you to shackle the block inside the hose. Clear vinyl hose lets you see the shackle.

TILLER COMB

A tiller comb is pretty much what it sounds like: A blade on the bottom of the tiller drops into the teeth of an upturned comb to hold the tiller in position. A convenient tiller comb is like an extra crewmember. It will hold the boat on course while you crank in the genny, adjust the topping lift, or nip below for a spot of tea. Well-balanced boats can sail for hours with the helm locked, which makes watch keeping much less tiring.

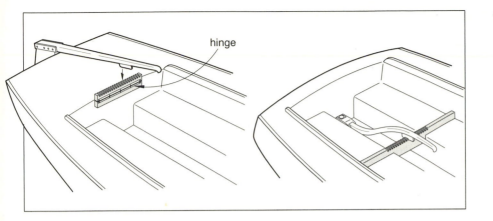

1 Determine the location of the comb. When the rudder is well aft, the comb can often be mounted to the aft end of the cockpit, hinged to fold down when not in use. When the rudder shaft comes up through the cockpit sole, a removable bridge is the more likely mount.

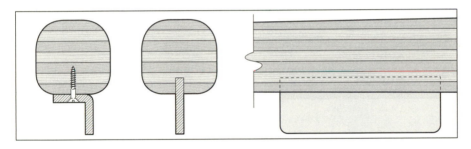

2 Based on the comb location, equip the tiller with the blade stop. The simplest is a length of angle iron screwed to the bottom of the tiller. You might also epoxy thin bar stock into a slot routed into the tiller. Since the tiller travels in an arc, the blade must be long enough to remain over the comb. A blade thinner than the kerf of your circular saw makes comb fabrication easier.

3 Use the stop as a guide to lay out the teeth. Placing the slots close together provides finer adjustment, but the thickness of the stock determines how thin you can cut the teeth and still have adequate strength. Remember that the angle of the teeth changes as you move away from the centerline. With the teeth marked on the blank, you should be able to cut them sufficiently accurately freehand with a circular saw. Make the comb as long as you like, but in use you are unlikely to ever want it to hold the tiller more than a few inches from the center position. (For heaving to, the tiller should be lashed.)

COACHWHIPPING

Of all the methods of wrapping a wheel, I find coachwhipping the most attractive. When done with strips of soft leather it provides an especially comfortable grip, but both canvas and braided line also give excellent results. If you plan to do this at home, be sure you mark the king spoke before you remove the wheel.

DOING THE MATH

The coachwhipping described here is done with six strips, and their combined width should be enough to completely enclose the rim. A typical wheel formed from 1-inch diameter tubing has a rim circumference of 3.14 inches (circumference = π x diameter), so each strip should be slightly wider than ½ inch. As a practical matter it is a good idea to give the strips a little extra width—say, ⅛ inch.

The length of the strips will be approximately twice the circumference of the wheel, so for a 30-inch wheel the strips should be about 5½ yards long:

$$\frac{(\pi \times 30 \times 2)}{36}$$

Continuous strips are ideal, but if joints are necessary they are easily hidden under the overlap.

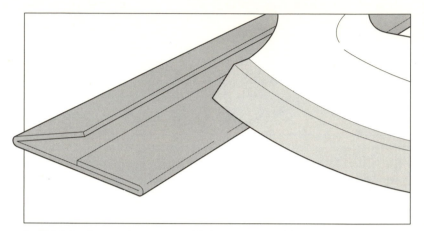

1 Thick leather can be cut to width, but canvas and thin leather must be folded on the edges. If you cut the strips twice their finished width, they will be the correct width when you fold the edges together. Pre-crease canvas by pressing it with a steam iron or rubbing the fold with the back of a knife.

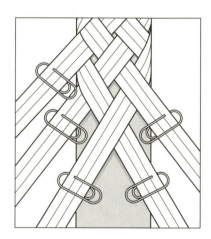

2 If you are using cord, lay multiple strands side by side to form the required "flat" strips. For example, for a 1-inch rim, use two strands of ¼-inch braided cord for each strip or, even better, three strands of ³⁄₁₆-inch braid. Paper clips over the groups of cords will help you keep them organized and flat.

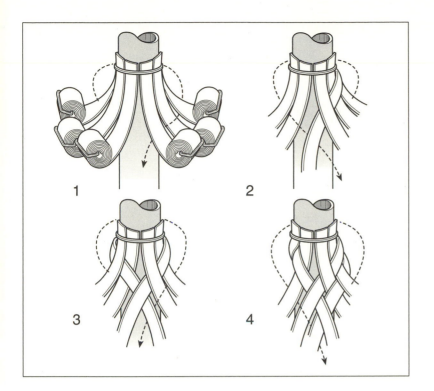

1

2

3

4

3 Roll up the strips and secure them with a tie, leaving a foot or so to start the whipping. Seize the strips to the rim at the king spoke, then follow the steps shown to get the whipping started. Continue right around the wheel, taking care to keep the weave as tight as possible. A rubber band tied around the whipping serves as a convenient movable clamp for the whipping already completed.

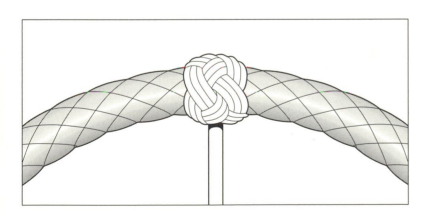

4 Seize the ends of the completed whipping and top it with a Turk's head knot. Canvas should be varnished (or painted) to seal it from dirt.

COCKPIT CHART BOARD

A chart near the helm is nearly always convenient and sometimes essential. But charts in the cockpit have a way of getting wet, scrunched, or blown away. Here is a solution guaranteed to please.

1 Cut two matching rectangles from ⅛-inch clear acrylic (Plexiglas). You can cut acrylic with almost any saw or buy it precut. The recommended size—18 inches by 24 inches—accommodates most charts folded twice. Round off all the corners and edges of the rectangles.

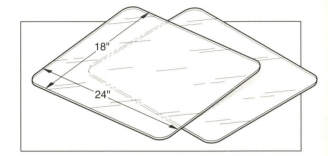

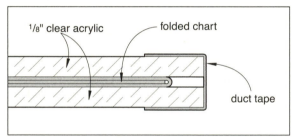

⅛" clear acrylic

folded chart

duct tape

2 Sandwich a folded chart between the two rectangles, then tape them together along one of the long edges to form a hinge, using heavy-duty duct tape.

3 Close the case with a pair of banker's clasps, available from any office supply store. This board lets you see both sides of the chart without removing it. With a pen-style marker you can make notations on the acrylic that will resist rain and spray, but will polish off with a dry cloth.

HAT/CHART CLIP

While you are at the office supply store buying banker's clasps, pick up a few bulldog clips. They have endless uses aboard a sailboat.

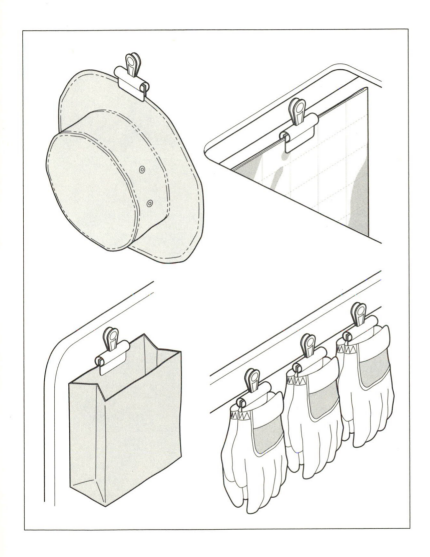

To avoid rust, sand the new clips, then give them a coat of zinc primer and a couple coats of paint. A clip screwed to the cabin bulkhead in the cockpit will keep your favorite hat aboard and handy. It can do the same for a loose chart. Mounted inside a cockpit locker, a clip provides dry chart storage that is also close at hand. A pad convenient for piloting notations might be clipped just inside the companionway. The clips also have dozens of nonsailing uses, such as holding a small garbage bag in the galley, outgoing mail by the companionway, or gloves in the anchor well.

COCKPIT CHART STOWAGE

If you prefer the simplicity of a loose chart to the chart board detailed on page 74, a stowage pocket in the cockpit will secure the chart and keep it dry.

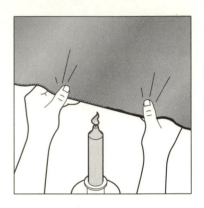

1 Start with a 19-inch by 29-inch rectangle of acrylic canvas, either cut with a hot knife or passed through a candle flame to seal the edges. Do not use vinyl; condensation wets the interior of a plastic bag in the sun.

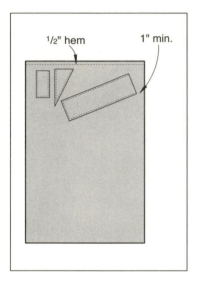

½" hem   1" min.

12"

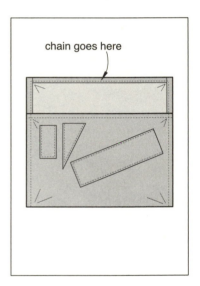

chain goes here

2 Sew a ½-inch hem in one end. This will be the top of the pocket front. Cut patch pockets to hold a pencil, dividers, and a plotter or parallel rules. Sew these near the top of the good side of the pocket front and at least 1 inch from the edge.

3 Fold the fabric 12 inches below the hem, putting the patch pockets inside, and seam both sides of the formed envelope. Place the stitches ½ inch from the edge.

4 Turn the envelope inside out. Because of the side seams, the sides of the flap are now folded over. Make this fold uniform and stitch it into a hem on both sides. Fold a hem into the edge of the flap, but slip an 18-inch length of brass (toilet bowl) chain into the fold before stitching. This will weight the flap closed.

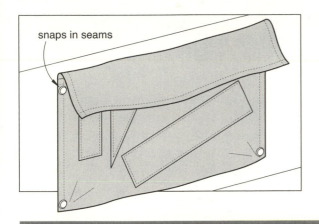

snaps in seams

5 Install snaps through the side seams near the top of the pocket. Install matching studs in the cockpit where you want the pocket. (Alternatively, you can mount the pocket with Velcro.) This pocket requires a twice-folded chart to be doubled but not creased.

BEAN BAGS

If you roll charts rather than fold them, you will wonder how you ever managed without these handy weights.

3"

1 Almost any soft, close-weave fabric can be used for chart weights. Old denim is ideal. Cut two 3-inch circles and sew them together—good sides inside—leaving about 1 inch unsewn. Turn them inside out through the opening.

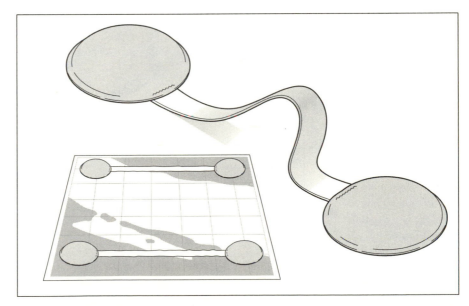

2 You can fill the bags with uncooked rice, but for tightly rolled charts you may appreciate the extra heft of lead shot. Pour the weight through the opening, filling the bag about half full. Joining a pair of bags makes them less likely to disappear, so fold under the edges of the opening, slip one end of a 12-inch length of webbing between the folds, and topstitch the bag closed. Attach a second bag to the other end of the webbing, then make a second pair. "Snapping" charts will be a thing of the past.

MINISPEAKER

If you're in the cockpit when your radio squelches to life in the cabin below, it is much like a page at the airport. Did they say *Lollipop?* At least with the engine running there is less confusion—because you probably can't hear the radio at all. Because the solution is so obvious—and so easy—it makes you wonder why so many sailors put up with this annoyance.

WHAT YOU NEED

A small speaker near the helm lets you monitor the VHF at a low volume. Chandlers sell waterproof bracket-mount extension speakers for about 20 bucks, or from an electronics outlet (such as Radio Shack) you can buy a mini-speaker that clips on. The speaker will come with several feet of wire and a plug, but you may need an extension and/or an adapter to fit your radio.

1 Because the speaker contains a magnet, be sure to mount it well away from the compass and the autopilot. For a permanently mounted speaker, get the wire below deck as near to the speaker as possible, then route it to the radio. It is perfectly fine to lengthen the wire by clipping it and soldering in additional speaker wire. Just be sure to stagger the connections and protect them with shrink tubing. Clipping the wire also simplifies feeding it below deck.

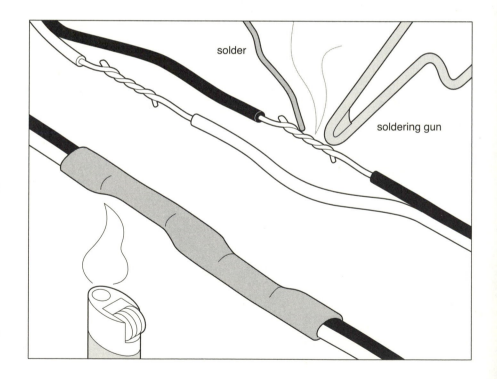

solder

soldering gun

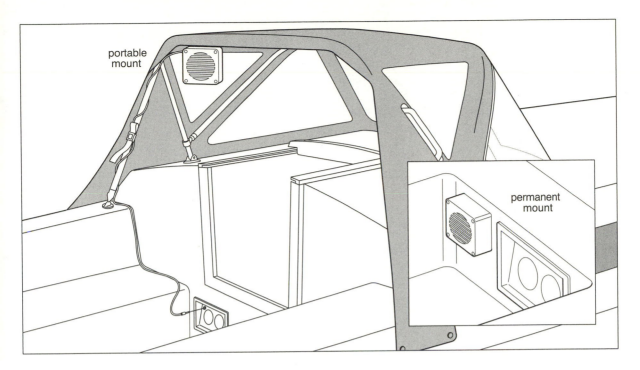

portable mount

permanent mount

2 A temporary speaker is more convenient when it connects to a plug in the cockpit rather than to the back of the radio. An extension that terminates inside a cockpit locker might be adequate, but a panel-mount plug will be better. Consider installing the plug in the engine panel if it is protected with a cover. Otherwise, inside a locker will be less corrosion prone than an exposed location.

EFFICIENT STOWAGE

A well-equipped sailboat, particularly a cruising boat, needs to carry an enormous amount of gear. Fortunately most boats feature a substantial amount of locker space—sometimes by good design, and sometimes just because the hull is round and the accommodations square. Either way, space is space.

When it comes to stowage space, more is better. But, of course, every extra cubic inch of hull volume dedicated to stowage is a cubic inch less of living space, so the roomier a boat is for a given hull size, the less stowage space it is likely to have. Every design is a compromise, and whether you will ultimately be happier with a larger living space or more locker space depends on how you use your boat.

For the most part the stowage enhancements in this chapter avoid this issue. They don't add stowage at the expense of accommodation. Rather, they typically make better use of existing cabinets and lockers. A cockpit locker cavernous enough to have an echo might be fine for stowing bags of sail, but try keeping anything else in it and you end up with a hopeless jumble in the bottom and nothing but air in the top. Cabinet interiors can be just as inefficient.

Requiring little more than a bit of wood or wire or fabric, the ideas that follow will help you get control of the jumble or make use of the dead space—or both.

LOCKER BAFFLES

"Divide and conquer." Apply this bit of military wisdom to the invading army of cans and equipment and you will emerge victorious—and a whole bunch happier.

THE STICK TRICK

How do you cut baffles to fit the contour of the hull? Easier than you think.

1 Whittle a point onto a flat stick—screen molding is perfect. Cut a piece of corrugated cardboard and tape it in the locker where you want the baffle, straight edges against the square sides of the locker. With the stick flat on the cardboard, position the point against the hull where the top corner of the baffle will be. Trace the edge of the stick and put matching marks on the stick and the cardboard. Call this number 1 and label it on both the cardboard and the stick.

2 Move the point of the stick down the hull a few inches and trace, mark, and number this new stick position 2. Continue moving the point and tracing the stick until you get to the bottom corner of the baffle. You can use a second stick if the first one becomes too long.

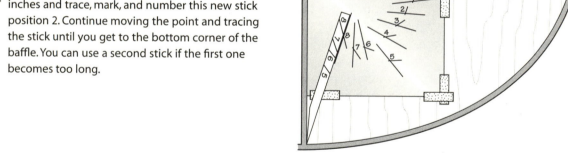
cardboard taped to bulkhead

3 Remove the cardboard and tape it to your baffle material with straight edges aligned. Put the stick back in position 1 and mark the point on the baffle. Mark positions 2, 3, and so on until a series of dots outlines the curvature of the baffle. Using a flexible batten, connect the dots into a smooth curve. When you cut on this line, the baffle will be a perfect fit.

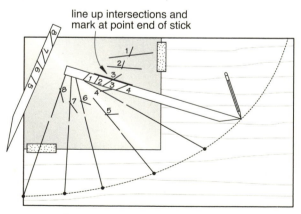
line up intersections and mark at point end of stick

MAKING THE DIVIDERS

As a rule of thumb, most lockers benefit from a baffle about every 12 inches. This limits the amount of digging, as long as you know which compartment the item you want is in. Even narrower compartments can provide the most efficient stowage for cans of similar size.

The best material for locker baffles is usually $\frac{1}{8}$-inch plywood. After you mark the contour with the pattern stick, cut the baffle and check it for fit. For better ventilation use a spade bit or hole saw to pierce the baffle with a pattern of 1- to 2-inch holes. Sand the baffle and paint it.

Three small wooden cleats set in thickened epoxy will normally be adequate to position the baffle. It is generally unnecessary to fasten the baffles; the contents of the locker will hold them in position. This also adds the flexibility of being able to easily reposition or remove a baffle.

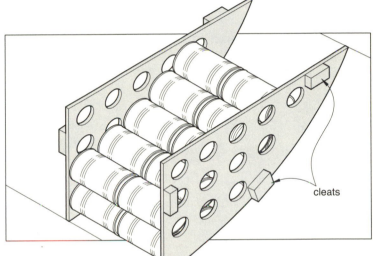

cleats

Sometimes a fore-and-aft baffle works well, dividing a locker into a deep inboard pocket and a shallow one outboard. Fore-and-aft baffles are as much shelves as dividers, so they should be cut from thicker plywood.

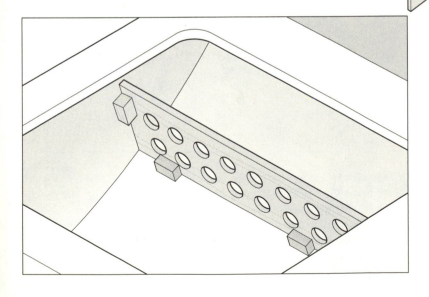

THE BASIC SHELF

No matter how much an owner complains about the scarcity of stowage space, open lockers on most boats and you will find them at least half empty. At home the same owner probably tosses a duffel up on a closet shelf. We don't tolerate wasted space in the top of a closet, and we have even more reason to use the space in the top of a locker. All it takes is the basic shelf.

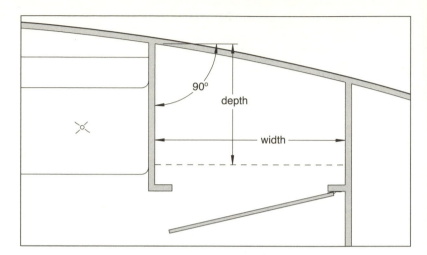

1 Where the shelf goes is determined by what you intend to put on it. Measure the width of the locker perpendicular to one side (front and back) and the maximum depth of the shelf. Shelves high in a locker typically do not come all the way to the front because of access. Unless weight is a major concern, 5-ply construction makes ½-inch plywood the best choice for locker shelves. Cut the plywood to the measured dimensions.

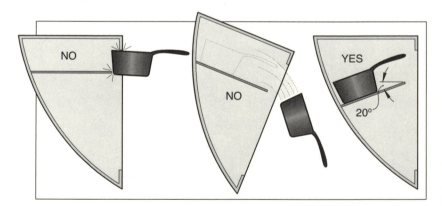

2 Ripping a 1 x 2 down the center makes inexpensive cleat stock for shelf mounting. Cut the stock to make one side cleat and tack it temporarily to the side of the locker. A "level" shelf will empty itself on one tack unless you give it a high fiddle. (Be sure there is room above the fiddle to pass whatever you want the shelf to hold.) However, if you slant the shelf down in the back about 20 degrees, there won't be any risk until the heel exceeds 30 degrees.

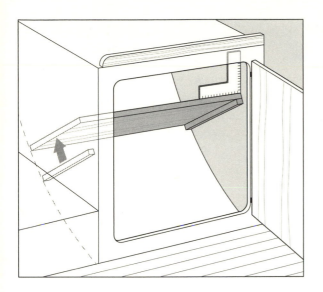

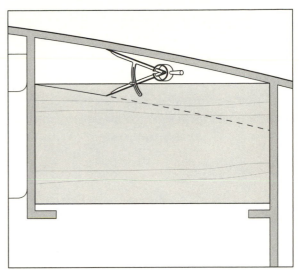

3 Put the shelf on the cleat and square it with the side of the locker to mark the position of the second cleat.

4 With the second support tacked to the locker, install the shelf and trace the hull contour onto it with a compass. For a shelf that is the full depth of the cabinet, you will have to use the pattern-stick method to trace the contour.

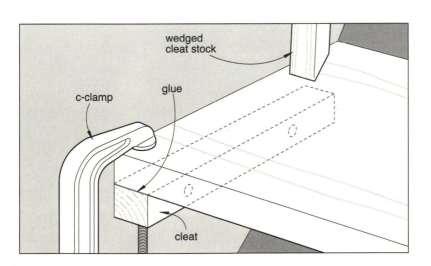

5 After you confirm the fit, screw and glue the cleats to the locker sides. Loose shelves are a bad idea on a boat, so glue the shelf to the cleats, clamping it in front and applying pressure in the back with a wedged length of cleat stock. If you want the shelf removable, omit the glue when you screw the cleats to the locker sides. For back support—not usually needed—epoxy a short cleat to the hull in the middle of the shelf.

FIDDLE RAILS

All shelves, whether you installed them or they came with the boat, need some kind of fiddle rail to corral their contents. Removable rails are the most versatile. Here is a montage.

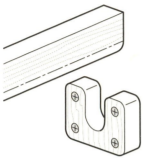

U-block. Sturdy, attractive, and among the easiest to make. Use a spade bit to bore a hole the width of the fiddle rail, then make two parallel saw cuts to the edge to create the U-shaped cutout.

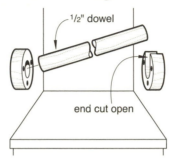

1/2" dowel

end cut open

Dowel. Easier than U-block. Cut disks with a hole saw, bore their center holes slightly larger than the dowel, then "open" one with parallel saw cuts.

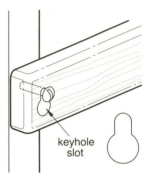

keyhole slot

Keyhole. Keyhole fiddles fit over screws into the front surface. Cut between two drilled holes to form the keyhole.

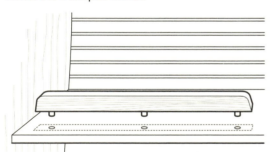

Peg mount. Peg-mount fiddles attach directly to the shelf. Bore holes through the shelf and into the fiddle. Glue pegs into fiddle.

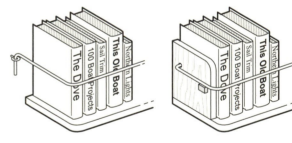

Wire. The easiest of all. Bend from ¼-inch brass, stainless steel, or aluminum rod. Install in drilled holes or like a latch hook. A stop may be needed to position the rail.

Fiddle net. Netting is ideal for a shelf containing small items. When attached at the back, the net can be dropped behind shelf contents when not in use. Sew the front edge around webbing and snap it *inside* the shelf lip.

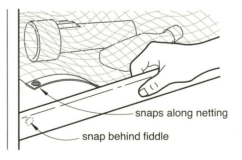

snaps along netting

snap behind fiddle

NET SHELVING

You can make the basic shelf with a sewing machine instead of a table saw. Net shelving is ideal for light items like paper products, and it provides maximum ventilation for clothes and towels and linens. Net shelves convert the waste of a hanging locker into a useful bureau with only the addition of cup hooks.

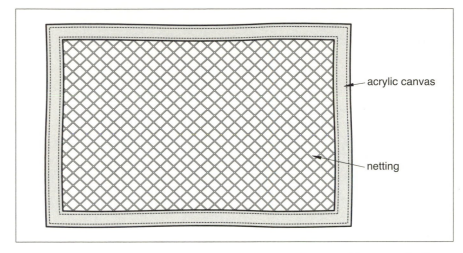

acrylic canvas

netting

1 Strong cotton or nylon netting provides the best ventilation and least weight, but use Phifertex (the vinyl-coated polyester mesh popular for outdoor furniture) for shelves that might contain small items. Cut the net to size and sew the perimeter inside a strip of folded acrylic canvas.

2 Install four or more cup hooks or L-hooks inside the locker, then install corresponding grommets in the canvas hem of the shelf. Net shelves are easily repositioned or removed for varying requirements.

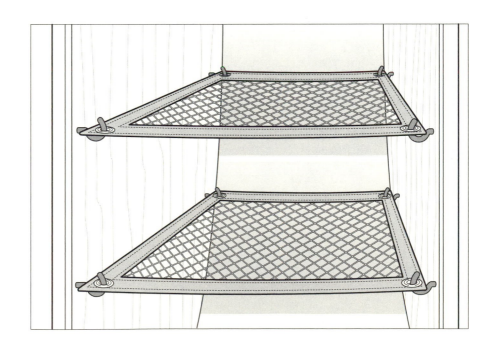

WIRE RACKS

With a supply of small-diameter brass, aluminum, or stainless steel rod, and two pair of pliers, you are limited only by imagination. Choose the material and diameter to suit your needs.

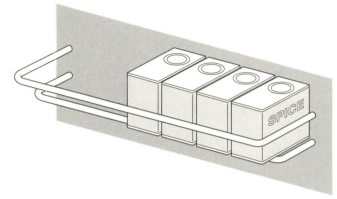

Horn or canister holder. Bend the upper loop slightly larger than the canister diameter, the lower loop slightly smaller.

Spice rack. The upper and lower loops are identical except that the lower loop is only half the upper loop's distance from the mounting surface. For tall spice containers, use two upper loops.

Binocular rack. Twin loops make a very secure binocular rack.

Camera holder. Cameras don't do well sliding around on a shelf. Here is an easy rack that keeps your camera secure and instantly accessible. The pull-out "latch" is optional.

Brush hook. Hanging brushes protects the bristles from damage.

Clothes rod. Shore clothes benefit from hanging before wearing them. If you have filled the hanging locker with shelves, a rod overhead in the forepeak beats turning the main salon into a Marrakech bazaar.

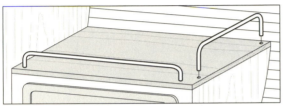

One more fiddle rail. A bent-rod rail can be installed permanently or fitted into the mounting hole only when needed.

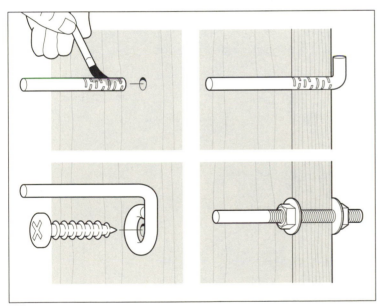

A sturdy bulkhead mount is achieved by notching the end of the rod with a hacksaw and gluing it into a tight-fitting hole using epoxy thickened with colloidal silica. Thinner mounting surfaces may require the addition of a wood block behind. For a stronger mount, push the rod through the bulkhead and bend a retaining hook on the end before setting the rod in epoxy. You can also thread the ends and bolt the rack to the bulkhead. For surfaces with no rear access, you may have to form loops for mounting screws.

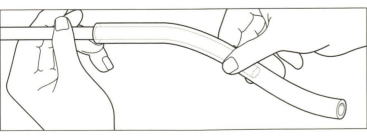

Sliding clear aquarium tubing over the rod will make racks easier on the surface of the items they contain.

COMPACT-DISC STORAGE RACK

You might make a wire rack similar to the spice rack to hold compact discs, but unless the rack is full the discs can spill through the bottom. A solid bottom is better. Discs should be shelved like books; space is too precious for separation between the cases. Their uniform size allows us to design an easy-access rack that won't spill its contents until the mast gets below horizontal.

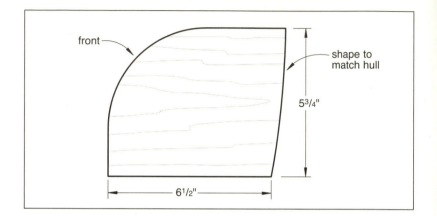

1 Cut two side pieces from either wood or acrylic. The front top corner can be plain or fancy, and the back can be contoured if necessary (for hullside mounting), but measured from the bottom rear corner the pieces should be 6½ inches wide and 5¾ inches high.

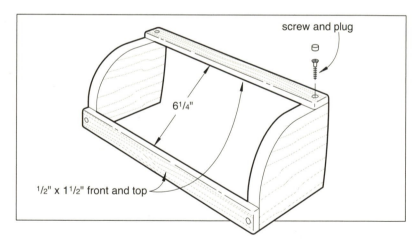

2 The width of the rack is determined by where you plan to install it. A rack 12 inches wide will hold about 30 CDs. The front and top pieces are 1½ inches wide and about ½ inch thick and should be cut to the planned inside width of the rack plus the thickness of both side pieces. Assemble the pieces as shown using thick acrylic cement if you are using acrylic, or epoxy for wood. Mechanical fastenings—either brass brads or screws—will strengthen the wood joints. Counterbore screw holes so they can be plugged.

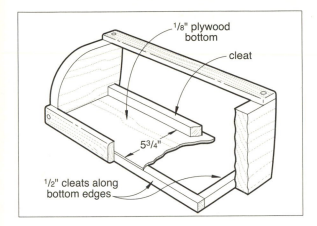

1/8" plywood bottom

cleat

5³/₄"

1/2" cleats along bottom edges

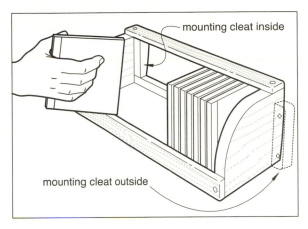

mounting cleat inside

mounting cleat outside

3 Glue ½-inch cleats to the sides and front flush with the bottom. Cut the bottom piece to size from ⅛-inch acrylic or plywood and glue it to the top of the cleats. Glue a full-length piece of cleat stock to the *top* of the bottom 5¾ inches from the front fiddle. This keeps the CDs from sliding back in the rack.

4 Mount the rack with cleat stock fastened to the inside of both sides. Inside mounting cleats prevent the removal of the outermost CD without first taking out the one next to it, so if that seems an intolerable inconvenience, put the mounting cleats on the outside. CDs in the rack cannot come out without the outside edge being lifted clear of the fiddle. The stop on the bottom makes it easy to tilt the cases on either side so you can grip the one you want.

CHART RACK

Keeping a couple of charts under your bunk is fine, but if you sail very far, pretty soon your accumulation of charts will give you a backache. Here are three better methods of chart stowage.

UNDER THE BUNK

When a bunk has drawers in the face, often there is enough dead space above the drawer to build a chart box.

1 With a saber saw and a thin, plywood blade, cut an access hatch the size of a full chart, half chart, or quarter chart, depending on the available space. Epoxy ¾-inch cleat stock half exposed around the perimeter of the cutout to form the support lip for the lid.

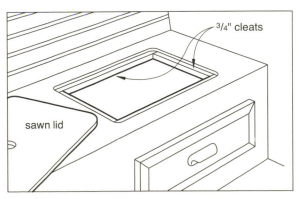

3/4" cleats

sawn lid

2 Frame the lip with 1 x 2 (or 1 x 3 if you have the room) epoxied to both the underside of the bunk and the cleat stock. Glue ⅛-inch plywood to the 1 x 2 frame to complete the box. Hole-saw large drainage holes in each corner of the plywood so a deck leak can't become marinade. Cutting the holes before you install the bottom will simplify clamping.

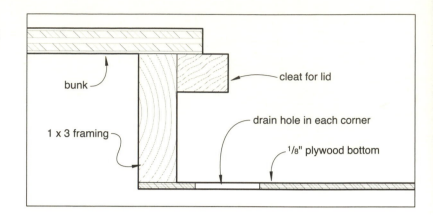

bunk

cleat for lid

1 x 3 framing

drain hole in each corner

⅛" plywood bottom

UNDER THE BUNK, TOO

If access to the underbunk space is through the top, chart stowage is still viable but you need a lift-out case.

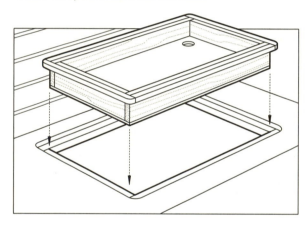

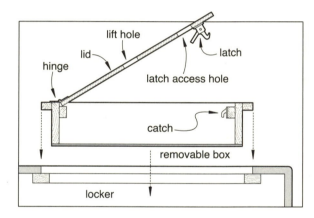

lift hole

lid

hinge

latch

latch access hole

catch

removable box

locker

1 Enlarge the opening to the maximum practical size and put a lip around it. Using ½-inch stock for the sides and ⅛-inch plywood for the bottom, build a box (complete with drainage holes) that will just slip into the opening. The depth of the box depends on how many charts you anticipate stowing. Frame the top edge of the box with cleat stock the thickness of the bunk so the box hangs flush in the opening.

2 Frame the inside of the box with cleat stock to support a new lid. Hinge the lid to the box on one side and install a bird catch on the other. For access to the locker, lift the lid as normal and the chart case comes out with it. For access to the charts, release the catch.

BULKHEAD RACK

If you have two or three feet of open bulkhead space, you can consider a vertical chart case. The dimensions here are for a rack holding about 25 charts folded twice on the same axis, but the case could be taller and narrower for cross-folded charts, and deeper for more charts. Use the wood of your choice.

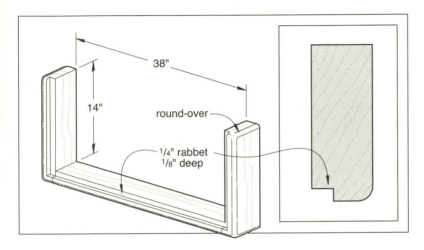

1 The three sides of the case are 1 x 2 screwed to the bulkhead, with the bottom piece butt-jointed inside the side pieces. Rout a radius on the outside edges and a rabbet $\frac{1}{4}$ inch wide and $\frac{1}{8}$ inch deep on the inside. The rabbet hides three edges of the plywood front. Cut the front piece from $\frac{1}{8}$-inch hardwood plywood to fit loosely in the rabbets.

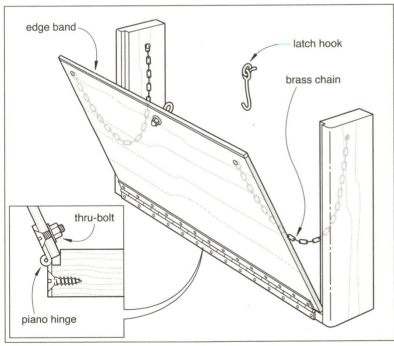

2 Edge band the top of the front. Fasten one side of a piano hinge to its bottom (using short machine screws) and screw the other side to the bottom of the case. A latch hook in the middle of the door and brass chains attached to the sides complete the case.

DROP-DOWN BINS

Here is an idea borrowed from commercial airliners: If headroom allows it, overhead space under the side decks can be converted to useful storage space with drop-down bins.

1 Fashion plywood boxes with a solid wood front panel. As an alternative to building the bins, you might find inexpensive wooden boxes in an import store, adapt prefabricated drawers, or even use plastic storage boxes or wire baskets (perfect for fruits and vegetables)—with or without adding a wood front. Join the back of the bin to a length of cleat with a piano hinge and fasten the cleat to the underside of the deck.

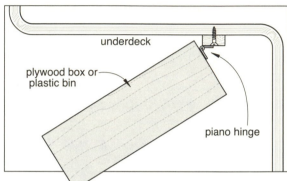

2 Attach an inch-tall molding to the overhead just in front of the closed bin(s). This hides fit imperfections and provides for easy latching. Mount barrel bolts on both sides of the bin and drill matching holes in the molding for simple, strong, and secure closure.

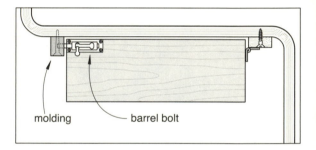

SLIDE-OUT COCKPIT STOWAGE

The high space in cockpit lockers, especially away from the lid openings, is almost always unexploited. Slide-out baskets let you use this space. You might also employ slide-out bins to take advantage of extra space above a quarter berth.

WHAT YOU NEED

You can make bins or use plastic tubs with molded lids, but for ease and light weight, nothing beats the runner baskets in the slide-out basket systems home stores sell for kitchen and laundry. Discard the frame and use the baskets one behind the other rather than stacked. Beyond baskets or bins, you need only a straight length of pine 2 x 4 for the rails.

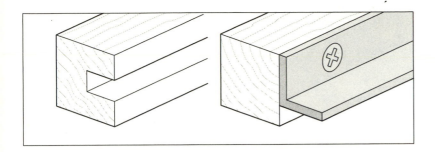

1 Rip the 2 x 4 to form two square rails. Use a table saw a circular saw to cut a channel in each of the rails for the basket runners. If you are using bins or tubs, screw angle aluminum to the rails as runners.

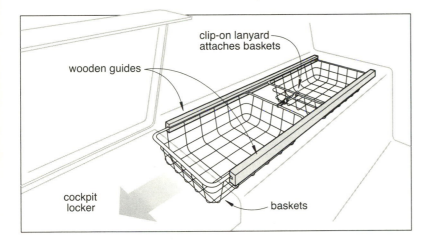

clip-on lanyard attaches baskets

wooden guides

cockpit locker

baskets

2 You can mount the rails with screws through the deck, but cleats fiberglassed to the underside (with epoxy resin) avoid defacing the deck and/or the potential for leaks. Screw the rails to the cleats, taking care that they are parallel. Connect each basket to the one behind with a short lanyard and a snap hook so they pull out like a train.

TABBING

ATTACHING A BULKHEAD OR A CLEAT to the hull with fiberglass is called tabbing. There are two rules: Always grind (meaning sand) the hull where the tabbing will be attached, and always use epoxy resin.

Position the bulkhead and use a disk sander to grind both the hull and the underside of the deck at least 2 inches on either side of the mount location. Also sand the bulkhead. Thicken some epoxy into a paste and glue the bulkhead into place. To avoid creating a "hard spot" in the hull, it is advisable to place a strip of foam (Airex) between the bulkhead and the hull. Hold the part in position with tape until the epoxy kicks.

Complete the installation by laying fiberglass tape into the joint on both sides of the bulkhead and saturating it with epoxy resin. Notch the tape to make it follow the contour of the hull. Two layers should be adequate.

Grind first and use a good grade of epoxy, and the item will remain attached until you take a chisel to it.

STACK BINS

A series of cubbyhole-like bins installed in the forward end of a cockpit locker can provide organized stowage for blocks, winch handles, vang tackle, deck plate keys, flags, and whatever else you want to keep in them. Opening aft, they are un-affected by heel.

You can construct the bins from plywood or, as shown here, adapt inexpensive stackable plastic vegetable bins for this use. Trim the legs on the bottom bin to get it to sit level in the bottom of the locker, then bolt or screw it to the bulkhead it sits against. Stack as many bins as possible on the first one, fastening each to the bulkhead. You can install a second tier, and perhaps even a third, against the first one. Using a variety of colors can make it easier to remember which items belong in which bins.

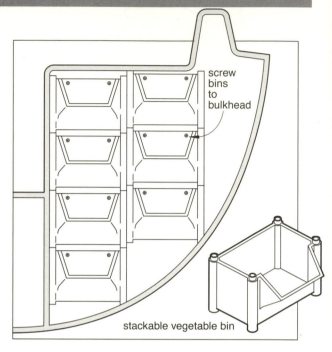

screw bins to bulkhead

stackable vegetable bin

HULL-SIDE STOWAGE

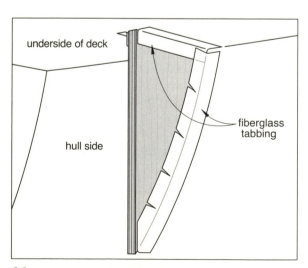

underside of deck

hull side

fiberglass tabbing

The wedge shape of hullside lockers means the space high on the hull is empty unless the locker is entirely full. This isn't a problem with shallow spaces, but in deep lockers, like those in the cockpit, this space is wasted.

1 Cut shallow kneelike partitions from ½-inch ply-wood—about 10 inches wide at the top. A partition about every 20 inches divides the bin into conve-nient compartments. Tab the knees to the hull and the underside of the deck with epoxy and fiberglass tape.

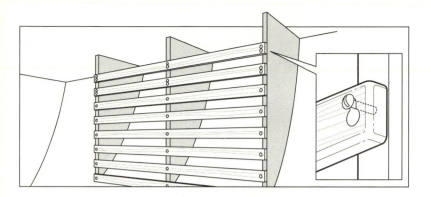

2 Screw and glue thin wood slats to the vertical edge of the knees. The top slat or two should be removable for wider access. This is a good place to employ the keyhole fiddles detailed previously.

COCKPIT LOCKER FLOORS

The sloped hull can be an inconvenient surface for flat-bottomed stores like boxes, bins, and jugs. It is also uncomfortable for standing (or squatting) when engine access is through the cockpit locker. Flat "floors" solve these problems without wasting any space.

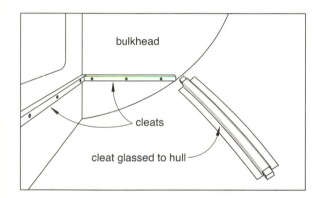

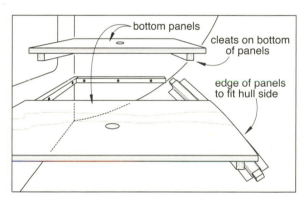

1 In a locker with a solid fore-and-aft bulkhead, a screwed-on 1 x 2 cleat will provide support for the floor. Lockers open to the engine compartment—blocked off by a removable partition—usually require the installation of a plywood stringer to support the inboard edge of the floor. In either instance, the outboard edge sits on cleats glassed to the hull.

2 Cut the floor panels from ½-inch or ¾-inch plywood. They sit loose on the perimeter supports, held in position by short cleats fastened to their underside. Divide floors into two or more panels to facilitate getting them through the lid opening and to allow access to the "cellar" without taking everything out of the locker. Oblong handholds ease lifting and handling. The space beneath the floors is ideal for seldom-used items like spare parts, extra hose, scrap wood, and the like.

DRAWER TRAY

A s with deep lockers, deep drawers tend to drag small items to the bottom like the legendary "under toad." Here is how to keep little items on top.

1 Decide how deep you want the tray and glue ¼-inch square stock all around the inside of the drawer that far below the top. Cut a piece of doorskin to fit inside the drawer on the cleats. If the tray is large, laminate two thicknesses.

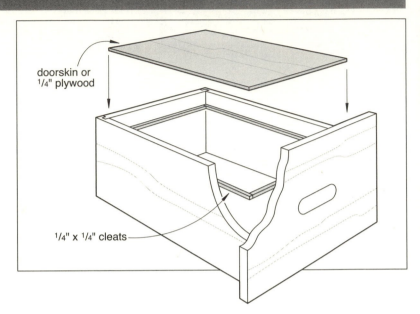

doorskin or ¼" plywood

¼" x ¼" cleats

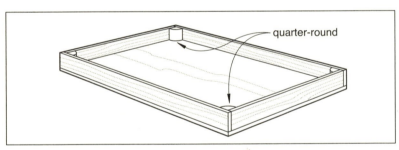

quarter-round

2 Cut the sides of the tray from doorskin and epoxy them into a rectangle, using ½-inch quarter-round molding in the corners. Glue the assembled sides to the bottom with thickened epoxy.

3 If you want dividers, cut them from doorskin, notching them where they intersect. Install a drawer pull in the center of the tray for lifting it. Rubber feet glued to the bottom will keep the tray from sliding around when you place it on a counter.

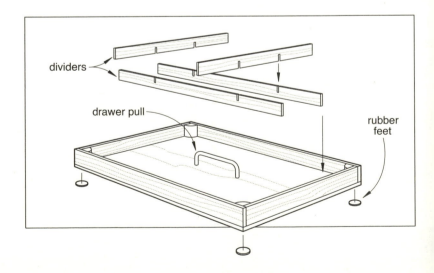

dividers

drawer pull

rubber feet

CLEAR POCKETS

Nothing organizes the little items on a boat better than clear pockets. They can hang against the hull, on the inside of cabinet doors, even out in the open. You can buy multipocket organizers, usually advertised for jewelry, but with a yard or two of heavy clear plastic and an equal amount of canvas, you can make your own that will be stronger and the right size for the location and the items you want it to contain. Always use your machine's longest stitch when sewing plastic.

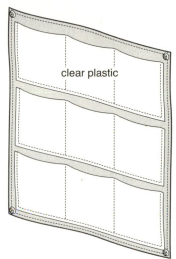

clear plastic

1 In its simplest incarnation, the pocket organizer is no more than strips of clear vinyl stitched along their bottom edges to a hemmed piece of canvas. Seams on both sides and a few intermediate rows of stitching close the ends and divide the strips into pockets. Add grommets to the four corners of the bag, or hang it with screws and finishing washers.

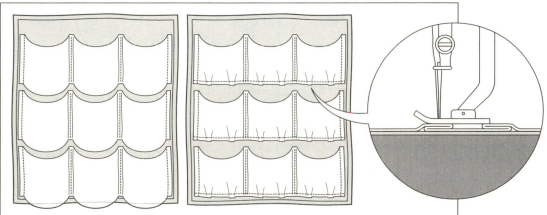

2 For larger items the pockets should be pleated at the bottom. Add about 4 inches *per pocket* to the length of the vinyl strips. Rather than sewing the bottoms of the strips, stitch their ends first. Divide the distance between the stitching equally on both the canvas and the plastic, then line up these division lines and sew along them. The vinyl should form uniform loops above the canvas. Pleat the vinyl closed at the bottom and sew across it. You can give your bags a more professional look by sewing binding tape around the perimeter, which also eliminates the need to hem the canvas blank.

BOAT CARE

For some it is a joy, for others a chore, but no matter which camp you're in, boat care is a requirement. Neglecting essential maintenance imperils both boat and crew and, as a stroll through almost any marina will attest, a boat that doesn't get regular upkeep soon looks shabby.

Most boat care is routine. Mast and rig require regular examination for signs of trouble. Fluid levels need to be checked before the engine is started, filters and oil changed on a regular schedule. Deck and hardware benefit from a freshwater wash—*salt is the enemy*—and the hull requires an annual application of antifoulant. Fuel lines are checked for leaks, sails are restitched, steering gear is lubricated, stuffing boxes are tightened, and wood is coated with oil or varnish.

Whether you want to do just enough maintenance to keep the stick up and the ocean out, or you are unhappy unless your boat glistens like a diamond, here are a few projects to help you get there with less effort. Use the time you save to go sailing, apply one more coat of varnish, or hoist a tankard in the club bar, as you see fit.

BRIGHTWORK COVERS: TILLER SOCK

Some would say the amount of time you spend sailing a boat varies inversely with the amount of wood on her deck. But even the most enlightened skipper is hard-pressed to deny the beauty of well-tended brightwork. Brightwork maintenance need not be onerous; protect your brightwork from the sun and you suspend corruption.

A tiller not only turns the rudder, it is your connection to the boat, a tactile link to the surge and tug of the ocean. When it isn't in your hand, protect its integrity—and its finish—with this simple canvas sock.

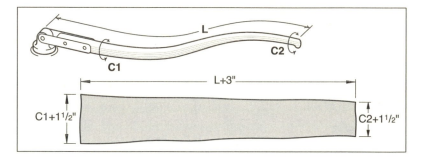

1 Measure the length of the tiller and the circumference at each end. Add 3 inches to the length and 1½ inches to the circumference measurements to get the dimensions for the fabric. Cut acrylic canvas to these dimensions.

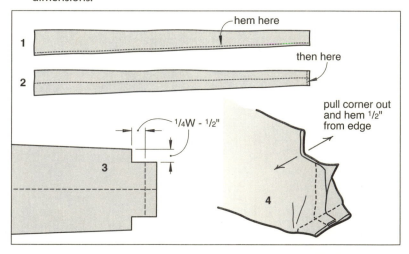

2 Fold the fabric good side in and seam the long edge. Refold to put the seam in the middle and stitch the narrow end closed. Measure the fold-to-fold width at the narrow end, divide it by four, subtract ½ inch, and use this number to mark square notches (measured from the folds and the end stitching) in both corners. Cut the notches, pull them open until they form straight slits, and seam them ½ inch from their raw edges.

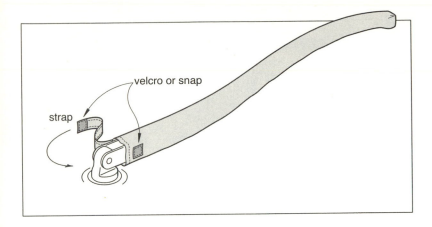

3 Slide the still-inside-out sock over the tiller to mark the finished length, then trim (if necessary), and hem the open end. Turn the finished sock inside out (a broomstick will help). It is a good idea to put a snap or Velcro strap on the sock to secure it.

BRIGHTWORK COVERS: HANDRAIL COVER

Almost all sailboats have wooden handrails on the cabintop. Sometimes they are the only wood on deck. In that case, pay a pro to lay on a foot-deep finish while you whip out canvas covers and you'll be all set.

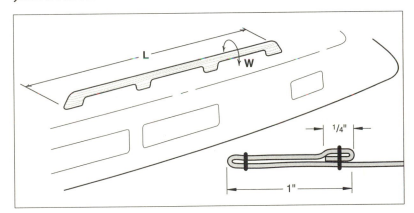

1 Measure the length of the handrail and the deck-to-deck distance over it. Add 3 inches to both measurements and cut a rectangle of acrylic canvas to these dimensions. Fold over each long edge ¼ inch, then 1 inch, and stitch these hems near both edges.

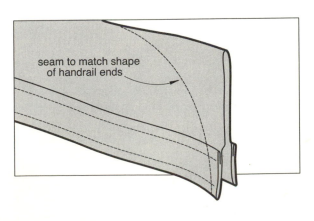

seam to match shape of handrail ends

2 Fold the cover in half with the hems outside and trace the approximate curvature of the end of the rail on the end of the cover. Sew this curved seam. With the cover still inside out, fit it over the rail and pinch the other end closed to position the end seam. Sew a matching curved seam on this end, taking care not to make the cover too short. Trim away excess fabric.

3 Turn the cover right side out and install snaps to fasten the sides together in the crook of the end standoffs. An intermediate snap or two is normally sufficient to hold down the center of the cover.

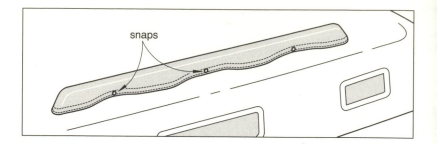

snaps

BRIGHTWORK COVERS: FIRE-HOSE CAPRAIL MAT

Sun is not varnish's only enemy. Abrasion destroys gloss and eventually penetrates the finish. A mat made of split fire hose protects the varnished rail where you come aboard—and it improves the footing.

FIRE HOSE

IF YOUR LOCAL FIRE STATION gives you 100 feet of hose and you use 3 feet to make a mat, don't throw the rest away. Canvas fire hose is tough and durable, making it useful elsewhere on the boat. Wrap it around anchor lines for excellent chafe protection. Use it to make gunwale guard for a hard dinghy, with or without foam underneath. (It can also take the sting out of the edge of a dock.) Stuff sections of the hose full of old rope, sew the ends closed, and install a pair of grommets to make cheap fenders. Tack it around the ends of a fender board to make an easy-on-the-deck workbench. Use it to make nonskid treads for the companionway steps. You still have 50 feet left, so use your imagination.

WHAT YOU NEED

Fire departments replace the hoses on their trucks regularly. If you will but ask, most are more than happy to load you up with as much hose as you are willing to carry away. Besides a piece of hose, all you need for the caprail mat is about a dozen snap fasteners and matching studs.

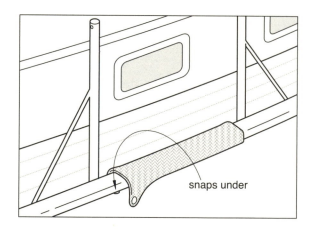

snaps under

Split the hose and cut a piece longer and wider than you want the finished mat. Hem all four edges. Install snaps in the side hems and corresponding studs under the rail on both sides.

BATTERY-MAINTAINING SOLAR PANEL

Nothing adds to battery life like keeping the battery fully charged. A charger can do the job at the dock, but there are real risks to leaving an unattended boat plugged in. A solar panel avoids this. On a mooring it is your only choice.

SIZING

Wet-cell batteries self-discharge at about 1 percent per day—more when it's hot, less when it's cold. So to *float charge* a 100-amp-hour (Ah) battery—that is, maintain a full charge—we need a solar panel with a daily output of about 1 Ah. Solar panels are rated in watts; divide by output voltage—14 volts is close enough for this purpose—to get the output current. Thus a 5-watt panel has a maximum output of about .35 amps. You can typically expect to average no more than 5 hours of ideal sunlight, so daily output of a 5-watt panel will be about 1.75 Ah.

Allowing for recharging inefficiencies, this is still about 50 percent more than necessary to float a 100-Ah battery. A good rule of thumb is 3.5 watts per 100 Ah of battery capacity. But throw in an occasional sunless day, put blocking diodes in the circuit, and let the bilge pump run once in a while, and 5 watts will be about right. A little extra capacity won't damage the batteries as long as you maintain the water level in them. Whatever size panel you select should have at least 33 cells for adequate voltage to fully charge the battery.

MOUNTING

Solar panels give maximum output when they are perpendicular to the sun's rays, but since boat movement makes inclining the panel toward the sun less than a sure thing, it is almost always best to mount the panel horizontal. It should not be shaded by booms, masts, or rigging since even the thin shadow of a shroud can drastically cut the output of the

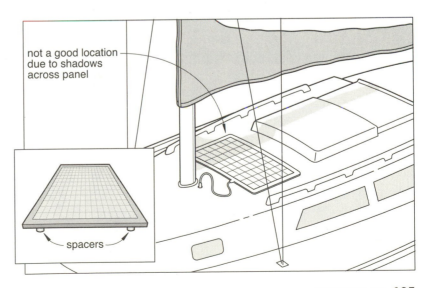

not a good location due to shadows across panel

spacers

panel. Heat also reduces output, so deck-mounted panels should be raised enough for free circulation beneath.

WIRING

Solar panels with a maximum output current of no more than about 1 percent of battery capacity don't need regulation. What is essential is a fuse close to the battery, since without it a short in the wiring is a dead short across the battery, with fire a likely consequence. A blocking diode to keep current from flowing back to the panel at night is not really needed, but if you are floating two battery banks with a single panel, diodes in both positive legs of the circuit keep the batteries isolated. Low-loss Schottky diodes are best.

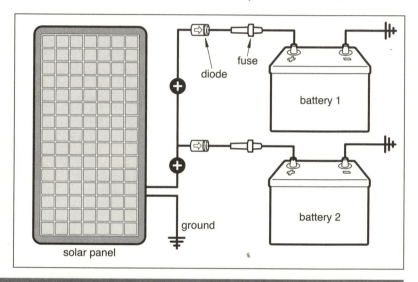

HYDROMETER HOLDER

For a couple hundred bucks you can install a so-called "E-meter" to electronically monitor your batteries, but you get a better picture of battery condition from a $2 hydrometer because it measures each cell individually. With one stowed near the batteries, checking cell condition becomes a natural adjunct to checking the water level. Regular cell monitoring results in better charging practices and provides an earlier warning of a battery's impending demise.

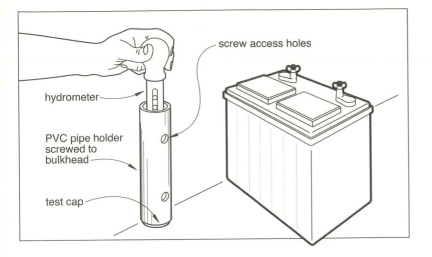

screw access holes

hydrometer

PVC pipe holder
screwed to
bulkhead

test cap

The holder is a piece of PVC pipe that is a slip-fit for the hydrometer you want to keep in it, excluding the bulb. Cut the pipe long enough to protect all the glass and the rubber tip. Close the bottom with a test cap. Drill two mounting holes with two larger holes opposite for inserting the screwdriver. Mount the holder vertically or diagonally.

STUFFING-BOX WRENCH RACK

There is only one place you use stuffing-box wrenches. Why, one might wonder, wouldn't you just keep them there? Good idea!

For bulkhead mount, cut a 2 x 2 block about 8 inches long. Bore two holes in the block slightly larger than the wrench-handle diameter. For flat-handled wrenches, drill two holes and cut between them with a coping saw to form an oblong slot. Position the holes far enough apart so that the wrench heads can't clink together. Use screws or bolts to mount the rack in an out-of-the-way location but within reach when you are fully contorted to adjust the packing nut.

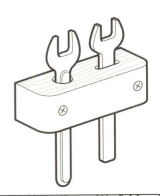

A bilge rack may be more out of the way and more convenient. In this case, shape the ends of the block to bridge the bilge either above or below the shaft tube. Be absolutely sure the rack won't restrict access to hose clamps, gudgeon bolts, or anything else. Grind the hull and epoxy the rack in place with a single layer of fiberglass tape over the ends.

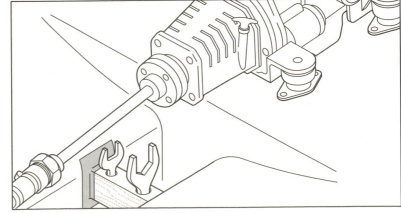

ENGINE ROOM TOOL STOWAGE

Packing-nut wrenches aren't the only tools aboard that see most use in a specific location. You need a particular wrench to bleed the fuel system, and probably a particular screwdriver to change the water-pump impeller. In fact, odds are almost every time you climb into the engine compartment, you use the same three or four wrenches, the same two screwdrivers, and maybe the oil-filter wrench. Having these tools where you need them saves two steps—digging the tools out and putting them back. It is false economy to take wrenches from the set in the toolbox; buy duplicates to keep here.

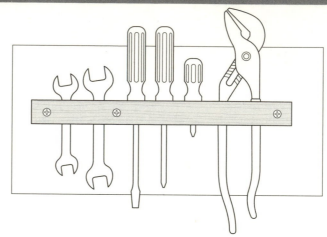

A rack mounted in the engine compartment offers the most convenience. A custom rack is easily fashioned from a length of pine with holes drilled, sawn, or routed to hold a limited array of tools. If the water pump is on the opposite side of the engine from the fuel system, two racks will probably be more convenient.

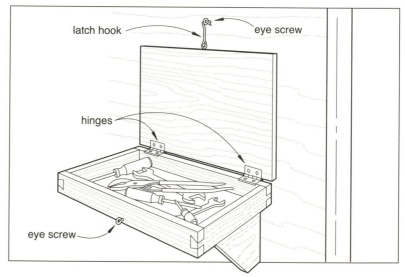

A box is more secure and somewhat more versatile. A flat box—essentially an enclosed shelf—offers easiest access. Whether the box is dovetailed mahogany or crudely constructed from 1 x 2 and plywood is up to you, but be sure it is mounted below eye level, the lid has a positive latch, and the bottom is supported with shelf brackets.

DRIP BASIN

Fuel that spills when you change the primary fuel filter or drain water from the bowl not only gives the cabin an unpleasant odor, it inevitably dribbles down the hull into the bilge, contaminating bilge water and making overboard discharge illegal. Even if you won't get caught, it isn't the right thing to do. Here is a simple solution that may make you slap your forehead.

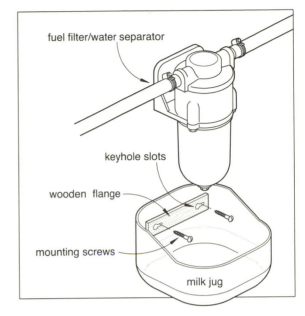

Cut a plastic milk jug as shown, and through the flange drill two holes large enough to pass the heads of the mounting screws. The plastic isn't rigid enough to support a keyhole mount (see page 82), so you will need to fabricate a "latch" from a wood strip with keyholes near the ends. Mount the drip tray far enough below the filter that it won't interfere with changing the cartridge.

A lift-out tray made from a plastic storage box can be somewhat more convenient. Purchase a 5-inch by 10-inchrefrigerator box (or whatever size suits your particular situation) and build a 1 x 2 frame to support its lip. Mount the frame to the bulkhead beneath the filter. An alternative to the wood frame is a bent-wire rack (see pages 88–89). Simply lift the box out to pour up drainage or spills for proper disposal.

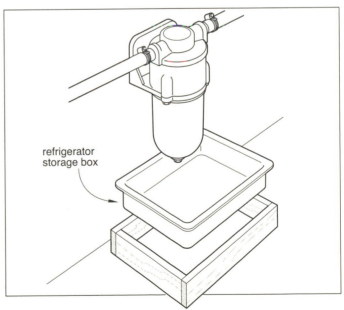

OIL-CHANGE PUMP

Almost everyone dreads the mess of changing oil, and as a result most of us put it off. Diesel engines are particularly hard on lubricating oil, and going longer between oil changes leads to mechanical failures and shorter engine life. Install this rig on your boat and you can change oil in your white linen suit if you like.

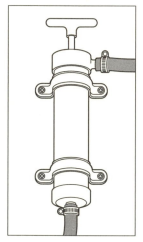

1 You need a small brass hand pump, like the Par Handy Boy. If your engine came with a pump, use it. Use pipe straps to mount the pump rigidly to a bulkhead and reasonably close to the dipstick tube.

2 Bend ¼-inch rod into a rack that will securely hold a plastic milk jug and install it convenient to the pump's outlet. Cut the outlet hose to extend inside the jug about 3 or 4 inches, and secure the hose to the pump with a hose clamp.

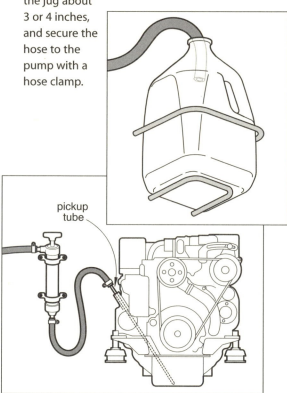

3 Buy about 15 inches of ¼-inch (ID) copper tubing from your local hardware store and carefully straighten it so it will slide inside the dipstick tube. With this pickup tube fully inserted, connect its top end to the pump inlet with an appropriate length of hose. Some adapting of the pump fitting may be needed. Clamp both ends of the hose.

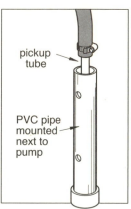

pickup tube

PVC pipe mounted next to pump

4 Finally, cap one end of a length of PVC water pipe and mount it next to the pump to contain the pickup tube when the pump is idle. Now changing the oil is simply a matter of inserting the pickup tube into the hot engine and operating the pump. The oil is transferred into the milk jug. When the pump sucks air, return the pickup tube to its sheath, pour in fresh oil, and carry away the full milk jug, replacing it with an empty. No muss, no fuss.

ENGINE ROOM FAN

This fan isn't for the engine; it's for you. Having air blowing over you when you do maintenance makes it easier to give a job the time it needs. Both engine and disposition benefit.

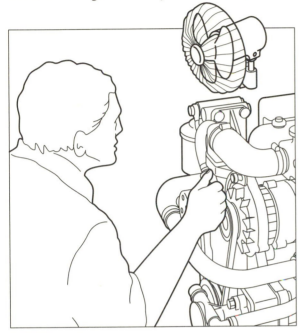

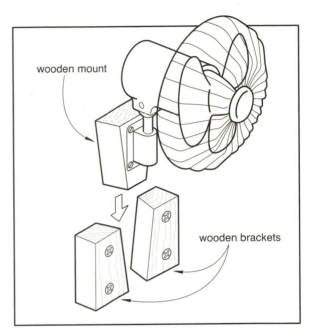

No need for an expensive fan here. An oscillating dashboard fan from a discount auto supply store is perfect. Mount it where it will draw in outside air and blow it in your face. A lighted switch is a good idea so you don't forget to turn it off.

If the best position for keeping you cool puts the fan in an otherwise inconvenient location, install the fan on a wedge mount. With two bracket sets, you can run the fan where it does the most good and store it where it is least in the way. Additional bracket sets will let you move the fan to another area of the engine compartment.

ENGINE ROOM LIGHTING: DROPLIGHT

Aside from making engine maintenance easier, good light also makes it easier to spot subtle signs—a rust stain, a film of oil—that can help you head off bigger problems.

A fixed light in the engine compartment casts only shadows on most of the engine. You can hold a flashlight in your teeth, but a hardwired droplight as a permanent feature of the compartment provides infinitely better light and is easier on the jaw.

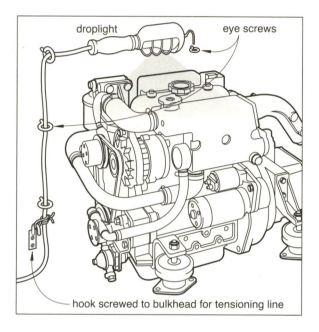

droplight   eye screws

hook screwed to bulkhead for tensioning line

A regular automotive droplight is easily converted to 12-volt use by cutting off the plug and installing a standard-base 12-volt (25-watt) bulb. Hang it above the engine and route the wire through fairleads (screw eyes will serve) to the electrical panel. A strop of light line slipped over a hook keeps the wire taut when the light is in its stowed position, but releasing the strop allows the light to be taken to any part of the engine.

ENGINE ROOM LIGHTING: SKYLIGHT

Natural light, when you can get it, is always superior to battery-powered lighting. Sunlight is also free. Unfortunately, letting it into the engine compartment isn't. But natural illumination makes such a difference to the comfort of the engine compartment that you are unlikely to begrudge the expense.

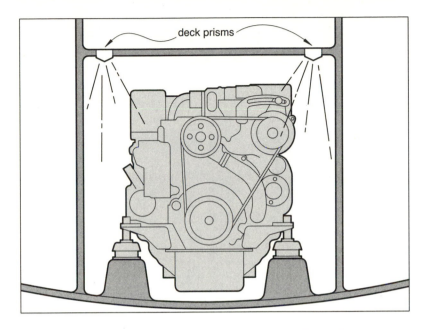

deck prisms

Twin deck prisms are ideal, but if you are unable or unwilling to buy two—they cost more than $100 each—the effect of a single well-positioned prism can be nearly as dramatic. Install the prisms through the cockpit sole and on either side of the engine. Place a single prism to the side of the engine where most maintenance takes place, not directly above the valve cover.

THE EXTRA TOUCH

Once in a while you go aboard a boat and some feature catches your attention. Maybe it is the innovative employment of knotty pine instead of teak, or the use of aromatic cedar in the hanging locker. Maybe it is how the pots are stowed in the galley or the ingenious installation of an exhaust fan above the stove. Or perhaps it is a cast bow fitting or carved tiller.

Custom boats are loaded with such features and they evoke admiration, maybe even envy. By comparison, most production boats are far less inspiring when they leave the factory. But even production boats become custom boats after a few years. Whether the added features are improvements depends on the style and perhaps the skill of the owner. If a boat has sweet lines, there is little reason you can't make a true yacht out of her.

The projects in this final chapter don't properly fit any of the previous categories. A few are less about using your boat and more about how you feel about her. Some are included for their contribution to appearance. Others are included for their innovation.

PICTURE HANGERS: VELCRO

Covering cabin bulkheads with framed art or other wall decor personalizes the interior of your boat and makes it more inviting, but regular picture hangers don't work on a boat. The best mounting practice can be to run screws right through the frame, one on each side, centered. But maybe you don't want to damage the frame, or the bulkhead. Here are two alternatives.

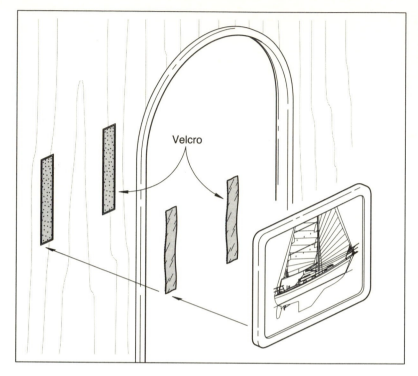

Velcro will support almost any frame, but the motion of the boat could tear heavier items like plaques or half-models free. Glue full-length strips of hook tape to both sides of the frame on the back. Remove any paper covering in the way and attach the Velcro to the frame with contact cement. Glue matching strips of loop tape to the bulkhead. Bulkhead surfaces, especially plastic laminate, should be sanded where the cement will be applied, but if you don't want to mar the surface, at least wipe it well with acetone. Roll the Velcro with a rolling pin or a glass to improve the glue bond.

PICTURE HANGERS: HINGE

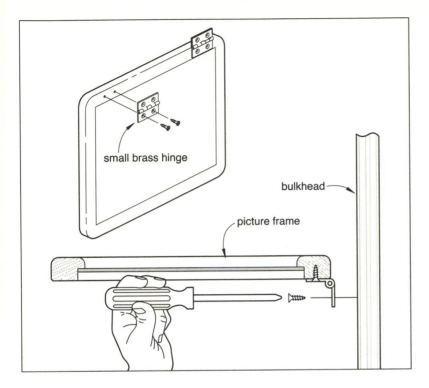

small brass hinge

bulkhead

picture frame

A pair of small brass hinges make an excellent picture hanger. Screw them to the back of the frame an inch or two from the sides. Level doesn't apply in a boat, but when you screw the other half of the hinges to the bulkhead, take great care to get the edges of the frame parallel to nearby straight features. A couple of squares of foam mirror tape (double-sided) keep the bottom of the frame against the bulkhead.

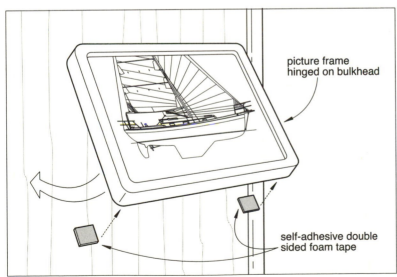

picture frame hinged on bulkhead

self-adhesive double sided foam tape

PLANT HOLDERS

Plants do well in the high light level of a boat and add to the warmth of the cabin. Here is a montage of ideas for a seagoing garden.

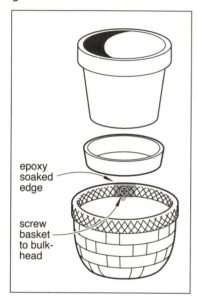

epoxy soaked edge

screw basket to bulk- head

Baskets are cheap, come in endless variety, and make excellent plant holders. Saturate a small area near the top with thickened epoxy to fuse the weave; then when it cures, put a screw through this spot to attach the basket to a bulkhead. Set the plant's pot and saucer inside.

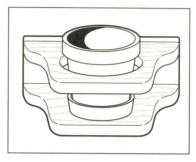

Teak and plastic drink holders sized for insulated drinks can also hold potted plants. The only trick is to match the pot to the holder.

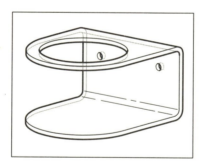

Because it is unobtrusive, bent acrylic is ideal for plant holders mounted under portlights. Start with a rectangle of ¼-inch acrylic 1½ inches wider than the pot and about 3 diameters long. Round the corners and use an adjustable hole cutter to put a pot-size hole in one end. Using a strip heater (see page 34), put two 90-degree bends in the acrylic to complete the holder.

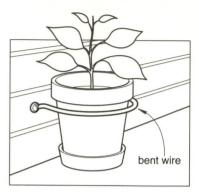

bent wire

Bent wire can also be employed to secure plants. This is an especially good way to corral plants on shelves and counters.

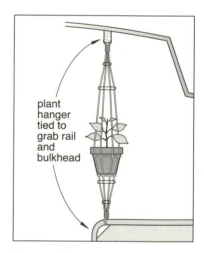

plant hanger tied to grab rail and bulkhead

Ropework hangers can work at anchor, and even underway if the hanger can be guyed to prevent it from swinging. They are readily available from plant sellers, or apply your marlinespike skills to make your own.

It is hard enough to get a note pad to stay put on my work desk. On a boat note paper is a disaster. Unless . . .

A fixed pad is comfortable to use only if it is shoulder level or higher. If your boat has a convenient high cabinet, this little enhancement will be one of the most appreciated. The pad can just as well be located on the door of a cabinet as on the side.

1 Just above the planned pad location, saber saw a 3-inch horizontal slit and smooth all edges with folded sandpaper. Inside the cabinet use a short piece of dowel or tubing suspended from a pair of cup hooks to hang a roll of adding machine tape below the slit.

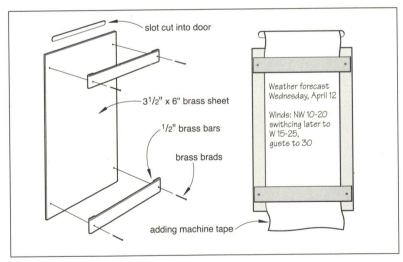

slot cut into door

$3^{1}/2$" x 6" brass sheet

$1/2$" brass bars

brass brads

adding machine tape

Weather forecast Wednesday, April 12

Winds: NW 10-20 swithcing later to W 15-25, gusts to 30

2 Cut a piece of brass sheet stock $3^{1}/2$ inches wide and at least 6 inches long; 8 or 9 inches is better if your location allows it. Cut two additional brass pieces about $1/2$ inch wide and 4 inches long and fold the ends under exactly $1/4$ inch. Round the corners of the big piece and temporarily tape it centered below the slit. Using brass brads, tack the strips in place near the top and the bottom of this brass writing surface, fastening both in the process. Thread the end of the paper through the slit and behind both crosspieces. The bottom one also serves as a tear edge.

ENDLESS NOTEPAPER: TILT-UP PAD

If your boat has no high cabinets, you can contain the
paper roll in a small hinged
box surface-mounted above
the pad. Or you can install it
in a low cabinet and give it a
tilt-up writing surface.

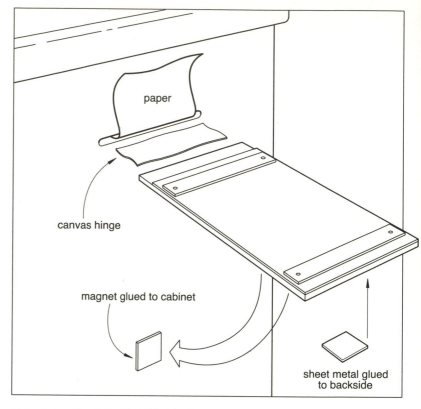

paper

canvas hinge

magnet glued to cabinet

sheet metal glued
to backside

Construct a tilt-up pad just like the fixed pad, except install the brass pieces
on a similar size piece of hardboard. Snip the brads and clinch them. Glue a
3-inch-wide strip of leather or folded canvas to the back of the hardboard,
feed it through the slot, and glue it to the inside of the cabinet to serve as a
hinge. If the pad is on a fore-and-aft surface, glue a refrigerator magnet to the
cabinet and a small square of sheet metal to the back of the hardboard to
prevent it from swinging out on one tack.

PENCIL HOLDER

Writing paper is no good without something to write with. Mount this simple pencil holder next to your endless pad.

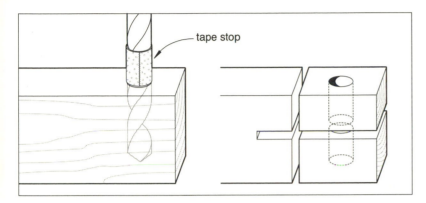

tape stop

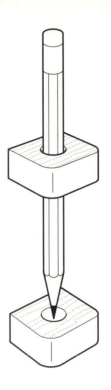

Wrap tape around a ³⁄₈-inch drill bit 1¼ inches from the tip, then use it to drill into the edge of a 1 x 2, taking great care to keep the drill perpendicular and not to drill beyond the tape stop. Center rip the 1 x 2 an inch beyond the hole, then crosscut the board on either side of the hole to yield two small blocks with center holes, one all the way through. Sand their outside edges, then glue the two blocks to the bulkhead, one 2 inches above the other. The top block should be at least 8 inches below any overhead interference.

BIKE-SEAT STOOL

If your boat has a dinette with seating on only three sides, or if it has a stand-up chart table, this idea may work for you.

WHAT YOU NEED

Start with a comfortable bicycle seat. If the one you select has a clamp bolt that requires a wrench, replace it with the kind you can turn by hand. From a junk frame you also need the tube the seat clamps to and the clamp that locks it to the frame tube. Finally, you need a piece of 1-inch galvanized water pipe, threaded on one end, and a threaded flange to fit the pipe.

1 Determine where the stool will go. The single leg can exercise tremendous leverage on the flange, so mounting it to the hull is much preferred over sole attachment.

Shim the flange to hold the pipe vertical, then bed it in this position with thickened epoxy. Grind the hull around the flange and use several layers of fiberglass and epoxy to secure it. Cut a pipe-size hole in the sole above the flange. You can give this hole a removable plug or a trim ring, but the unadorned hole will likely be the least noticeable.

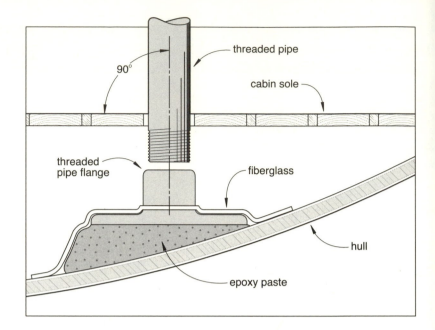

2 Slide the pipe through the hole and screw it into the flange. Assemble the seat to its support and use it to determine the appropriate height of the pedestal. Cut the pipe, then saw notches in the end so it can be clamped to the seat support. Adjustable height allows the same stool to be used for more than one purpose. The seat and pedestal are easily separated for convenient stowage.

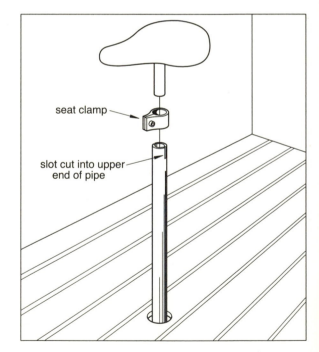

CEILING

Of all the methods employed to cover a fiberglass hull's raw inner surface, none is as classy as wood ceiling. Despite its expensive look, a wood ceiling in the forward cabin is amazingly easy to install, and the change it makes in the appearance of the boat is spectacular.

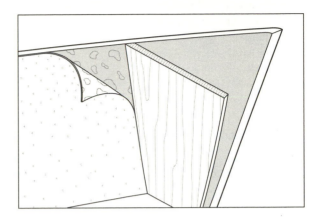

1 Start by removing the old covering and stripping the hull surface of paint and glue. This is typically the hardest part of the job, and you might elect to strip the hull only where the frames will go.

2 Rip ½-inch or ¾-inch strips (depending on the thickness of insulation you plan to install between the frames) from a length of one-by oak. Glue the frames to the cleaned and sanded hull with quick-set epoxy, one frame at each end and intermediate frames on 16- to 20-inch centers. Unless the curvature is excessive, ½-inch strips can usually be pushed flat against the hull; ¾-inch strips may need crosscut kerfs about halfway through the strip to give it adequate flexibility. Hold the frames against the hull with 1 x 2 and C-clamps as illustrated.

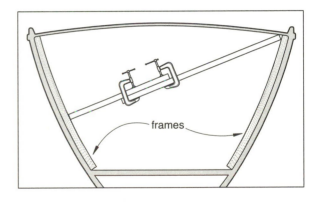

frames

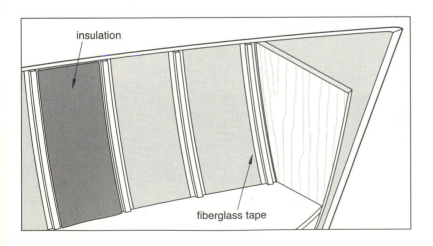

insulation

fiberglass tape

3 Cut 4-inch-wide strips of 10-ounce fiberglass cloth and cover the frames with one or two layers saturated with epoxy resin. When the resin cures, cut insulation (see page 125) to fit the spaces between the frames and lay the insulation in place.

4 With a table saw, a sharp smooth-cut blade, and a steady hand, you can rip slats from two-by stock. Otherwise have the slats milled to about ⅜-inch thick and 1½ inches wide. If you cut your own, sand them with a finishing sander. Rout a small radius on both front edges. You will cut them to length as you fit them.

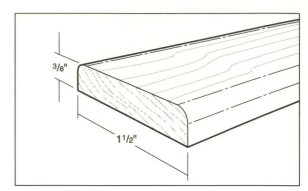

5 Varnish or oil the battens before you install them. Coating all surfaces avoids moisture intrusion from the back side. A couple of coats of epoxy resin under the varnish will provide the longest-lasting moisture barrier.

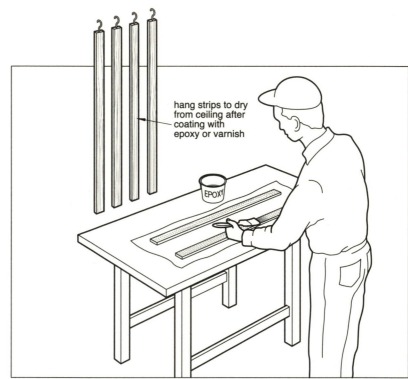

hang strips to dry from ceiling after coating with epoxy or varnish

6 Start with the top slat and trim it about ⅛ inch short of the bulkheads at either end. This allows for some expansion and avoids annoying creaking of the bulkhead moving against the end of the slat. Use spacers to put a uniform gap between the slats. This spacing, necessary in a wooden hull for ventilation, is more about tradition in a fiberglass boat, but it does keep the slats quiet. A quarter of an inch will probably look most pleasing.

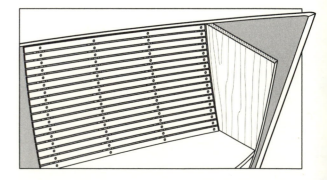

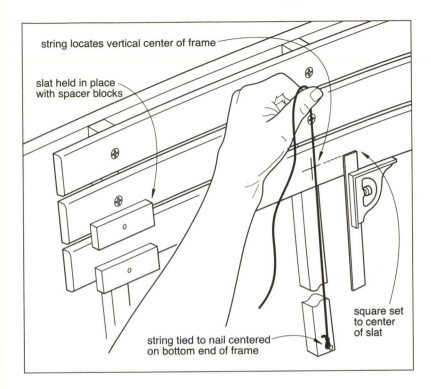

string locates vertical center of frame

slat held in place with spacer blocks

string tied to nail centered on bottom end of frame

square set to center of slat

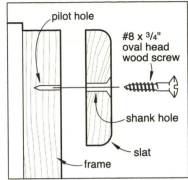

pilot hole

#8 x ¾" oval head wood screw

shank hole

slat

frame

For exposed screw heads, pilot-drill both the slat and the frame, then countersink the hole in the slat. Use #8 x ¾-inch pan-head screws—brass or stainless steel as you prefer.

It is essential to get the fastening screws in perfect alignment, so tack a string to the bottom center of every frame and pull it tight to the top screw each time you mark a screw location. The string will assure vertical alignment. Use a preset carpenter's square to position the screw in the slat's center. You can tack slats temporarily into position with a wire brad nailed through a short cleat and into the frame through the gap.

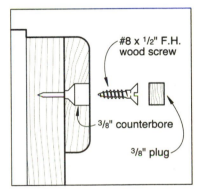

#8 x ½" F.H. wood screw

⅜" counterbore

⅜" plug

If you want the screws covered with wood plugs, bore the holes to a ¼-inch depth using a brad-point drill to assure a clean edge. Run a pilot drill the rest of the way through the slat and into the frame. Use #8 x ½-inch stainless steel screws. Set the plugs in varnish, trim them with a chisel, and sand flush. If the slats are varnished, touch up the plug and sanded area, then apply a fresh coat to the whole surface.

INSULATION

THE INSTALLATION OF WOOD CEILING provides the perfect opportunity to insulate the hull in the forward cabin. Various flexible insulation products are available from building suppliers that will eliminate hull condensation and make the cabin both warmer in cold weather and cooler in heat. The insulation need not be glued to the hull; the ceiling will secure it. If you select a product with a foil backing—a good choice with the bonus, some say, of giving your boat a brighter radar return—cover the foil with dark contact paper so it doesn't show through the gaps between the slats. The paper can go right across the frames.

PIG STICK

Flag etiquette requires a yacht club burgee to be flown at the masthead, but fewer and fewer boats are equipped for a masthead flag, so today the burgee is more often seen flying at the starboard spreader. Aside from being proper, a flag at the masthead gives a boat a jaunty look. But pig sticks—the not undescriptive name given to a masthead flagstaff—have a notorious reputation for fouling, banging, and sundry other mischief. Here is a trouble-free pig stick. If you don't have a club affiliation, fly your private signal (nice sound, that) from the masthead.

1 Opposite any masthead instruments attach a small cheek block to the side of the mast as close to the cap as possible. Reeve a ⅛-inch braided polyester halyard through the block and take both ends to a small cleat installed on the same side of the mast a few feet above the deck.

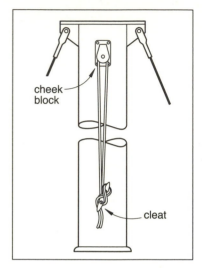

cheek block

cleat

2 Sand and paint or varnish a 3-foot length of ½-inch hardwood dowel. Take extra care to seal the ends. Bend a piece of stiff brass or stainless steel wire as shown. The straight side of the wire should be a couple of inches longer than the hoist dimension of the burgee. Drill a pilot hole in the end of the dowel and fasten the wire through the small loop, leaving the screw loose enough to allow the wire to rotate freely.

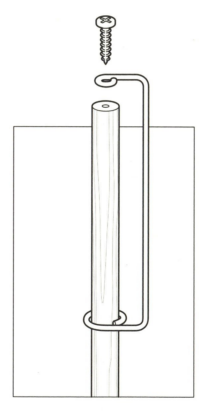

3 About a foot from the other end, drill a ⅛-inch hole through the dowel at a 45-degree angle. Drill a second 45-degree hole angled in the opposite direction about 2 inches from that end. This configuration raises the bottom of the burgee about a foot above the masthead, which is normally adequate to place it above masthead lights and instruments. If you require more height, use a longer (and perhaps larger) dowel.

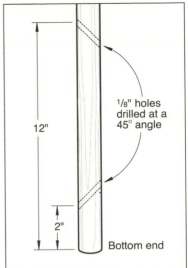

12"

⅛" holes drilled at a 45° angle

2"

Bottom end

CGSC

4 Lash the burgee to the wire, using rolling hitches on the wire to keep the lashings from sliding. To keep the stick quiet against the mast, slip a length of hose over it between the drilled holes, or apply a pair of whippings. Run the ends of the halyard through the angled holes, inserting them on the side where the holes are closest together, then tie them with a square knot. Keep the halyard tight as you hoist and the pig stick goes up vertically. Make both falls fast with plenty of tension to keep it that way.

CHAIN-PIPE PLUG

Anyone who thinks deck pipes don't leak has never taken green water over the bow. Usually the little cap just washes off, but even if it doesn't, the chain notch lets in plenty of water when it is submerged. Here is how to make it watertight—with the anchor still ready to go.

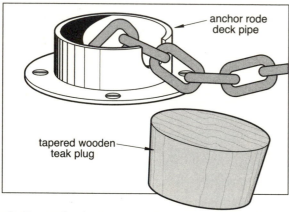

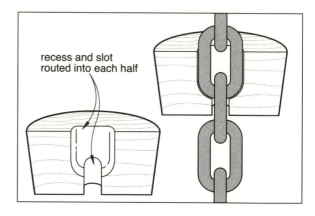

1 Empty the deck pipe and carve a tapered teak block that just enters the mouth of the pipe. This is much like the wood plugs you should have tied to every seacock. In fact, you could use a seacock plug in a round deck pipe, but teak stands up to the deck exposure better. The deck-pipe plug has to start oversize because you will lose width when you saw it in half.

2 Saw the plug in half. Then use a router and a chisel to notch both halves to fit back together over two links of chain. When you have a good fit, put the anchor and chain in the normal stowed position and clamp the plug over two links that fall a couple of inches inside the pipe. Epoxy the two halves back together over these two links. Seal around the chain link exiting the bottom of the plug with tape, then pour epoxy resin in the top to "pot" the chain inside the plug and make it watertight.

3 Finish shaping the plug to get a tight fit inside the deck pipe. The weight of the chain will hold it in place, but a good tug releases it when you need the anchor. Keep the metal cap to keep out rain when the anchor—and the wood plug—are on the bottom.

PORCH LIGHT

Most of us leave a porch light on when we expect to get home late so we won't be fumbling for keys and feeling for the lock in the dark. It makes good sense, so why don't we do the same on our boats, or at least have a light we can switch on when we first come aboard?

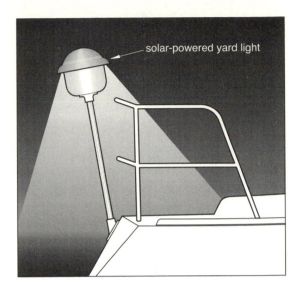

solar-powered yard light

For about $20 you can buy a solar-powered yard light intended to illuminate a walkway without the necessity for wiring. This same light, fitted into a flagpole socket or other support, will come on at dusk and illuminate your cockpit admirably for several hours. It draws no power from the ship's battery and can be left completely unattended.

on/off switch located inside cockpit pocket

light

outside switch (DPST)

battery

inside switch (DPST)

A shielded sternlight mounted below the bridge deck gives off lots of reflected light on a dark night without dazzling. If you prefer, you can install a low-draw "courtesy" light next to the companionway for more direct lighting on the lock. Install a waterproof switch in the cockpit, perhaps inside a coaming pocket or other protected location. For the price of an extra switch (both must be DPST), you can operate the light from the deck or the cabin.

COCKPIT SPEAKERS

Often the only place to permanently mount cock-pit speakers is the foot well, not the best place acoustically, and a pair of 5-inch holes through the topsides certainly doesn't improve seaworthiness. A lot of sailors settle on a boom box for music in the cockpit, but here is another option.

1 Select a pair of thin speakers. Waterproof (Poly-Planar) makes good sense for cockpit use. Duplicate your bottom dropboard from a pine plank and cut two mounting holes for the speakers, spaced as far apart as the length of the board allows.

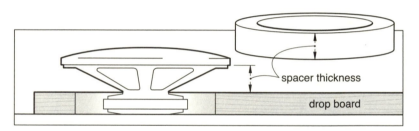

2 Rout wire channels in one side of the board. Lay the board on a flat surface and sit a speaker in one of the holes. If the mounting flange sits above the board, fabricate a round spacer to fill the gap. The mounted speaker should not protrude beyond the back of the board.

3 With the speakers mounted, run the wires in the routed channel, then cover the back of the board with plastic laminate (Formica) or doorskin. Solder the appropriate phono jack to the wires. When you want music in the cockpit, just drop this board in place and plug it in to your stereo. You can step over it to go below. The boat can also be closed up with the speaker board still in place—great for blasting Wagner when offshore weather turns dramatic.

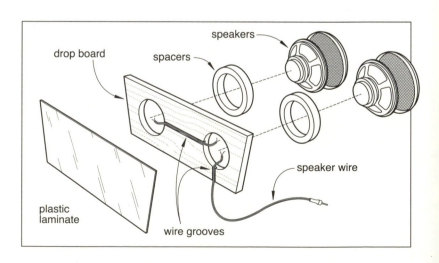

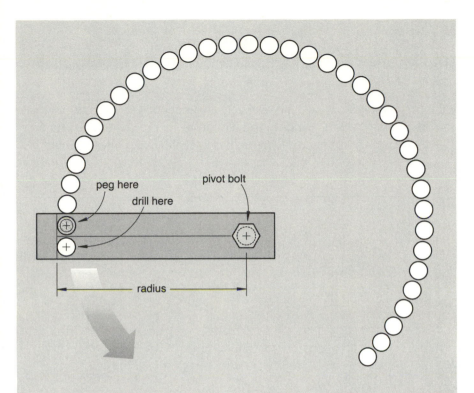

peg here

drill here

pivot bolt

radius

MAKING A ROUND CUTOUT

YOU NEED NOT BE INTIMIDATED by the prospect of cutting a large round hole. A simple-to-make jig makes round cutouts easy. Mild steel is the best material for the jig, but hardwood will serve. Drill two holes—¼ inch is a good size—side by side and nearly touching. Draw a line tangent to the outside edge of both holes and a second line perpendicular to the first and passing between the holes. Measure from the intersection along this line a distance equal to the radius of the hole you want to cut, and drill the pivot hole here. Drill the same size hole in the center of the cutout location and pin the jig in place.

Run the drill through one of the two guide holes and insert a peg. Drill through the second guide. Rotate the jig one hole, peg it, and drill again. Continue moving the peg and drilling until you end up with a perfectly circular pattern of holes. Cut between the holes with a coping saw and finish with a rasp if necessary.

FAUX DAVITS

A good hard dinghy is a joy. It is easy to row, fun to sail, and relatively dry under power. It can be dragged up a rocky beach or left against a seawall without concern, and it is mostly ignored by thieves. But a hard dinghy is a pain to carry. Davits are convenient but ugly. This rig is only slightly less convenient but almost invisible.

OFF-THE-SHELF HARDWARE

There are any number of ways to configure this dinghy lift system, including the use of custom-fabricated fittings, but the "davits" shown here use standard hardware available in any chandlery. The dinghy modification requires four 1-inch by 4-inch mast tangs. The standoffs are made from 1-inch stainless steel tubing, the same material used in Bimini top frames. You probably need about 3 feet, depending on transom configuration, and the heavier the wall thickness, the better. You also need two stainless steel rail base fittings, two top-frame jaw-slide fittings, and two eye ends, all to fit the tubing.

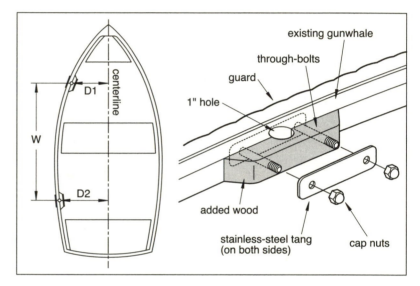

1 Prepare the dinghy by adding two 1-inch holes through the gunwale on one side—like oversize oarlock sockets. Widening the gunwale and adding thickness may be necessary. Sandwich the holes with through-bolted tangs to allow them to support the full weight of the upturned dinghy. The outside tang should be hidden by the gunwale guard. Locate the holes at least half the dinghy length apart; the closer they are to being equidistant from the centerline, the straighter the dinghy will be when it is turned up.

> **NOTE:** The proper place for a dinghy offshore is on deck. A dinghy on the transom, whether turned up or in real davits, is vulnerable to following seas. This system provides an easy means of dealing with the dinghy in protected waters, and it is a terrific way to keep the dinghy from banging against the big boat in tidal anchorages. Lifting the dinghy daily also avoids fouling and discourages theft. If you plan to stow it this way, be sure you install a drain plug in the bottom and open it to prevent the dinghy from collecting rainwater.

2 Mount the two rail base fittings on the transom of the big boat about 6 inches higher than the gunwale of the floating dinghy and exactly the same distance apart as the gunwale holes. These are the only visible modifications to your boat, but if they offend you, you can adapt through-hull fittings or glassed-in tubes as the standoff sockets. Shim the sockets as necessary to get a straight fore-and-aft alignment. They should be horizontal or tipped upward a few degrees. If the transom has significant rake, use angled base fittings. Through-bolt the fittings and use backing plates.

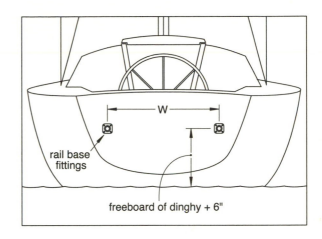

rail base fittings

W

freeboard of dinghy + 6"

3 Cut two pieces of tubing long enough to extend about 1 inch through the gunwale holes with a jaw-slide fitting attached. Drill a hole near the end of the tubing for a quick-release retaining pin. Cut two more pieces as the standoffs, making them long enough to reach just beyond the vertical plane of the sternrail when they are seated in the transom sockets. For a reverse transom, the standoffs need to be long enough to reach beyond the aftmost edge of the boat. Install the eye ends on the standoffs and bolt them to the slide jaws.

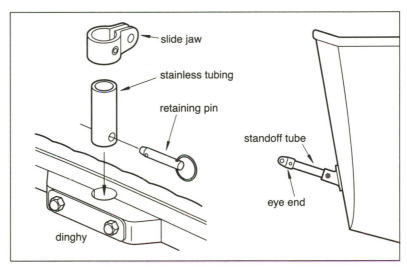

slide jaw

stainless tubing

retaining pin

standoff tube

eye end

dinghy

4 To hoist the dinghy, insert the hinged standoffs through the gunwale holes and insert the pins to keep them from pulling out. Lift the gunwale of the dinghy—either from the deck or by shifting your weight to the opposite gunwale—and insert each standoff into the transom socket. Use a tackle rigged from the backstay to the opposite gunwale to pivot the dinghy out of the water. A small amount of hoist lifts the bottom clear of the water for at-anchor stowage, or tilt the dinghy all the way against the transom for carrying it underway.

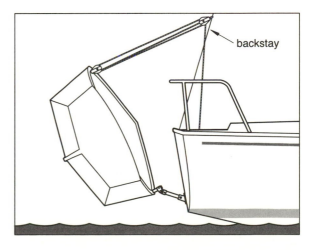

backstay

KEEL WHEEL

Here is another modification that adds convenience to the hard dinghy, saving both your back and the dink's finish.

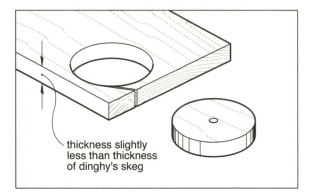

thickness slightly
less than thickness
of dinghy's skeg

1 Cut a roller from a hardwood plank slightly narrower than the width of the dinghy's keel. You can also use Lexan or other durable plastic. The diameter of the roller isn't critical, but the larger it is, the easier it will roll over soft surfaces.

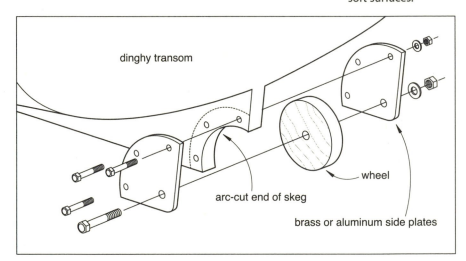

dinghy transom

arc-cut end of skeg

wheel

brass or aluminum side plates

2 Cut an arc into the aft end of the keel. Fabricate side plates from brass or aluminum sheet and bolt them to the keel. Pivot the roller on a ³⁄₈-inch bolt through the plates.

INDEX

A

Acrylic
  bins, 34–35
  canvas, 39, 76
  chart board, 74
  cutting board, 33
  plant holder, 118
  racks, 34–35
Alarm system, 12
Anchor light, 23
Anchor lines, anti-chafe wrap for, 104
Awnings, eyebrow, 54

B

Backrest, cockpit, 57–58
Baffles, locker, 82–83
Barrel bolt latches, 13–14
Baskets
  drop-down, 94
  plant, 118
  slide-out, 94–95
  See also Bins; Boxes
Batteries, charging, 105–106
Bean bag weights, 77
Berths, grate, 59–61
Bike-seat stool, 121–122
Bilge-pump light, 22

Bilge rack, 107
Binocular holders, 27, 88
Bins
  acrylic, 34–35
  drop-down, 94
  slide-out, 94–95
  stacked, 96
  See also Boxes; Racks
Blade stop, tiller, 70–71
Block-out curtains, 53
Blocks
  cleat, 69
  knife, 30
  silencers for, 70
Boat care, 101–113
  battery-maintaining solar panel, 105–106
  brightwork covers, 102–104
  drip basin, 109
  fan, engine-room, 111
  hydrometer holder, 106–107
  lighting, engine-room, 112–113
  oil-change pump, 110
  tool stowage, 107–108
Bolts, barrel, 13–14
Book rack, 35
Bow netting, 66
Boxes
  binocular, 27
  chart, 91–93
  cutlery, 32

  drop-down, 94
  mug, 31
  serving tray, 33
  tool, 108
  See also Bins; Racks
Breakers, circuit, 24
Brightwork covers, 102–104
Brush hook, 88
Bucket, canvas, 42–43
Bulkhead, tabbing of, 95
Bulkhead rack, 88, 89, 93
Bunk stowage, 91–92
Burgee, pig stick for, 126–127

C

Camera holder, 88
Canister holder, 88
Canvas
  acrylic, 39, 76
  bucket, 42–43
  coachwhipping, 72–73
Caprail mat, 104
Cassette rack, 35
CD storage rack, 90–91
Ceiling, wood, 123–125
  insulating, 125
Centrifugal pump, 44
Chain-pipe plug, 128
Chain scrubber, 45

International Marine/
Ragged Mountain Press   ✈

A Division of The McGraw·Hill Companies

10   9   8   7   6   5   4   3   2   1

Copyright © 1998 International Marine, a division of The McGraw-Hill Companies.

All rights reserved. The publisher takes no responsibility for the use of any of the materials or methods described in this book, nor for the products thereof. The name "International Marine" and the International Marine logo are trademarks of The McGraw-Hill Companies. Printed in the United States of America.

Library of Congress Cataloging-in-Publication Data
Casey, Don.
   100 fast and easy boat improvements / Don Casey.
        p.   cm.—(The International Marine sailboat library)
   Includes index.
   ISBN 0-07-013402-2 (alk. paper)
   1. Boats and boating—Maintenance and repair. I. Title.
   II. Series.
VM322.C36 1998
623.8'223'0288—dc21   97-32735
                                   CIP

Questions regarding the content of this book should be addressed to:
       International Marine
       P.O. Box 220
       Camden, ME 04843

Questions regarding the ordering of this book should be addressed to:
       The McGraw-Hill Companies
       Customer Service Department
       P.O. Box 547
       Blacklick, OH 43004
       Retail customers: 1-800-262-4729
       Bookstores: 1-800-722-4726

Visit us on the World Wide Web at www.books.mcgraw-hill.com

This book is printed on 60-pound Renew Opaque Vellum, an acid-free paper that contains 50 percent recycled waste paper (preconsumer) and 10 percent postconsumer waste paper. ♻

Illustrations for chapters 1, 2, 3, 6, 7 and chapter 5—figures 5-12 through 5-19—by Kim Downing
Illustrations for chapter 4 and chapter 5—figures 5-1 through 5-11, and figures 5-20 through
       5-28—by Jamie Downing
Illustrations for pages 6, 26, 46, 62, 80, 100 and 114 by Jim Sollers
Printed by R.R. Donnelly, Crawfordsville, IN
Design and layout by Ann Aspell
Production by Janet Robbins and Mary Ann Hensel
Edited by Jonathan Eaton and Nancy Hauswald

DON CASEY credits the around-the-world voyage of Robin Lee Graham, featured in *National Geographic* in the late sixties, with opening his eyes to the world beyond the shoreline. After graduating from the University of Texas he moved to south Florida, where he began to spend virtually all his leisure time messing about in boats.

In 1983 he abandoned a career in banking to devote more time to cruising and writing. His work combining these two passions soon began to appear in many popular sailing and boating magazines. In 1986 he co-authored *Sensible Cruising: The Thoreau Approach*, an immediate best-seller and the book responsible for pushing many would-be cruisers over the horizon. He is also author of *This Old Boat*, a universally praised guide that has led thousands of boatowners through the process of turning a rundown production boat into a first-class yacht, and of *Sailboat Refinishing*, *Sailboat Hull & Deck Repair*, *Canvaswork & Sail Repair*, and *Inspecting the Aging Sailboat*, all part of the International Marine Sailboat Library. He continues to evaluate old and new products and methods, often trying them on his own 29-year-old, much-modified, Allied Seawind.

When not writing or off cruising, he can be found sailing on Florida's Biscayne Bay.

THE INTERNATIONAL MARINE SAILBOAT LIBRARY

100 Fast and Easy Boat Improvements has company:

Sailboat Refinishing
by Don Casey
Hardcover, 144 pages, 350 illustrations, $21.95. Item No. 013225-9

Sailboat Hull & Deck Repair
by Don Casey
Hardcover, 144 pages, 350 illustrations, $21.95. Item No. 013369-7

Canvaswork & Sail Repair
by Don Casey
Hardcover, 144 pages, 350 illustrations, $21.95. Item No. 013391-3

The Sailor's Assistant:
Reference Data for Maintenance, Repair, & Cruising
by John Vigor
Hardcover, 176 pages, 140 illustrations, $21.95. Item No. 067476-0

Troubleshooting Marine Diesels
by Peter Compton
Hardcover, 176 pages, 200 illustrations, $21.95. Item No. 012354-3

Inspecting the Aging Sailboat
by Don Casey
Hardcover, 144 pages, 300 illustrations, $21.95. Item No. 013394-8